Richard Maier

Scrimshaw

In Theory and Practice

4880 Lower Valley Road • Atglen, PA 19310

Published by Schiffer Publishing, Ltd.
4880 Lower Valley Road
Atglen, PA 19310
Phone: (610) 593-1777; Fax: (610) 593-2002
E-mail: Info@schifferbooks.com

For our complete selection of fine books on this and related subjects, please visit our website at www.schifferbooks.com. You may also write for a free catalog.

This book may be purchased from the publisher. Please try your bookstore first.

We are always looking for people to write books on new and related subjects. If you have an idea for a book, please contact us at proposals@schifferbooks.com.

Schiffer Publishing's titles are available at special discounts for bulk purchases for sales promotions or premiums. Special editions, including personalized covers, corporate imprints, and excerpts can be created in large quantities for special needs. For more information, contact the publisher.

Other Schiffer Books on Related Subjects:
Scrimshaw, ISBN 978-0-88740-455-9
Advanced Scrimshaw Techniques, ISBN 978-0-7643-3017-9
Contemporary Scrimshaw, ISBN 978-0-7643-3049-0

ISBN: 978-0-7643-4967-6
Printed in China

Originally published as Scrimshaw-Gravur in Theorie und Praxis by Wieland, Bad Aibling ©2010 Wieland.
First Edition, 2010
Translated from the German by Omicron Language Solutions LLC
Photographs: Richard Maier, Hans J. Wieland, iStockphoto (pp. 11, 30, 31, 33, 35)
Design and Layout: Andreas Schleicher, Caroline Wydeau

CONTENTS

A FEW INTRODUCTORY SENTENCES

The ancient art of Eskimos and whalers has been brought back to life. Today, scrimshaw is a recognized art form that delights many collectors and is especially widespread among knife enthusiasts. Many fine knives—usually handmade unique pieces—are finished with scrimshaw work on the grip. But the art of scrimshaw has not been limited to knives for a long time.

Richard "Ritchi" Maier is one of the best and most well-known "scrimshanders" in Europe. This Austrian learned the trade of engraving at the famous school in Ferlach and is one of the most sought after weapon engravers internationally. He is known to knife enthusiasts through his long association with knife maker Egon Trompeter.

In this volume, he passes on his knowledge and vast experience in scrimshaw engraving. First, he explains the origins and history of scrimshaw, then deals with the different materials and tools before introducing the reader to the secrets of this art technique. He provides lots of tips for beginners and deals with common problems. Anyone who is interested can take up their needle and create scrimshaw engravings using this guide.

This book series presents a range of topics related to making knives in a way so that you understand each step and can also reproduce it. We place especial emphasis on practical aspects.

All volumes in the series are published with a spiral binding (more precisely, with a Wire-O binding). This way, the book will remain flat where you open it. We have also designed the size of the images and print so that you can read and recognize everything as you are working and have the book lying beside you.

We have tried to present every step as intelligibly as possible. Despite this, before you pick up any tools, you should carefully read the descriptions in this book. This way, you will know what is coming next and will not experience any unpleasant surprises during work.

I wish you much enjoyment and success in your engraving work!

Hans Joachim Wieland
Editor-in-chief, MESSER MAGAZIN

HISTORY

1.1 Stone Age Origins

Let us go back through the mists of time to humanity's roots and the beginnings of art. Carving signs and symbols into the teeth and bones of animals they had hunted was part of our ancestors' lives. Art as a cult was closely associated with hunting magic and rituals. Engravings on mammoth ivory are among the oldest works of art in the world and are silent witnesses to the artist's struggles with himself and his environment. The origins of ivory engraving lead far back into the Stone Age.

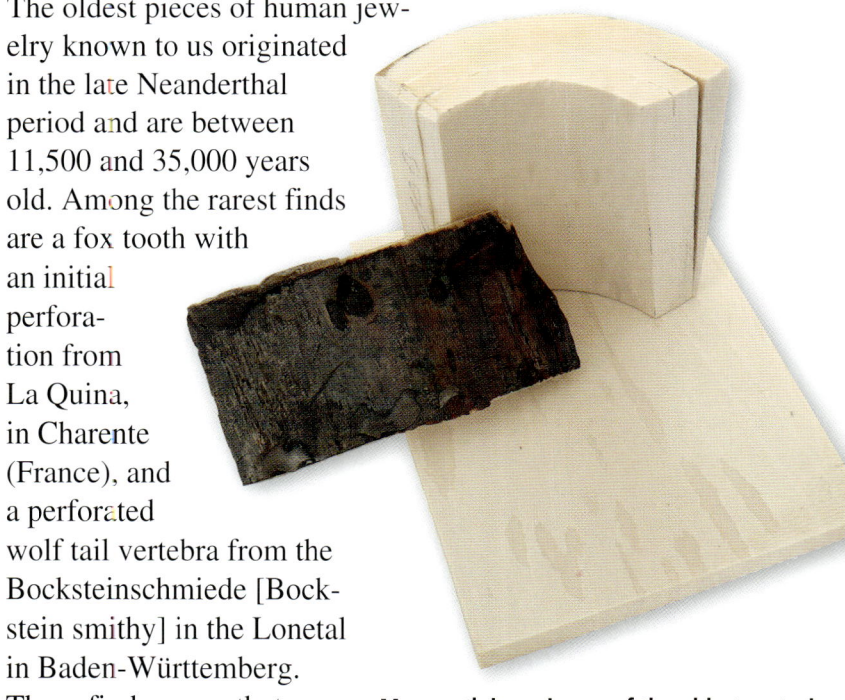

The oldest pieces of human jewelry known to us originated in the late Neanderthal period and are between 11,500 and 35,000 years old. Among the rarest finds are a fox tooth with an initial perforation from La Quina, in Charente (France), and a perforated wolf tail vertebra from the Bocksteinschmiede [Bockstein smithy] in the Lonetal in Baden-Württemberg. These finds prove that some Neanderthals were already wearing pendants made from bone as ornaments.

Mammoth ivory is one of the oldest materials mankind has used to express creative achievements. This raw material plays an important role in modern scrimshaw artwork.

MAMMOTH-HUNTING IN THE STONE AGE

Winter has arrived and the clan is living crowded together in tents under a high rocky shelter. Suddenly, the air is filled with penetrating, siren-like trumpeting that heralds the approach of a mammoth herd. The hunters are roused from their sleep. They pull on their furs and emerge from their tents to closely watch the silhouettes of the mighty pachyderms emerging in the foggy morning.

A look back to humankind's roots: art is closely associated with hunting magic and rituals.

The dominant male is over sixteen feet tall, with a big hump behind his head. His colossal body has stored incredible amounts of fat under his hide. His long coat, reaching to the ground, provides ideal protection against the cold. Two little balls of fur hanging close by their mothers add their voices to the herd chorus.

The men—at their observation posts—never let the animals out of sight for a moment. At first, they are still busy grazing: the long, curving tusks are used to scoop the grass free from under the thin blanket of fresh snow. With their flexible trunks equipped with a finger-shaped, mobile extension, they tear up the dwarf willows growing on the banks, sliding them in their huge mouths and crushing them with their powerful molars. You can hear the noise of their chewing from far away. They look like giant, mist-shrouded masses of wool.

The herd has again started on its trek and moves deeper into the valley. The hunters are happy, because they are aware of the pitfalls at the end of the small woods, well camouflaged beneath the snow ...

Ornaments and hunting have always been closely intertwined. The oldest ivory pendants include small button-like oval finds with double perforations from the Geißenklösterle cave at Blaubeuren and animal figures from the Vogelherd cave (in the Heidenheim area) in Baden-Württemberg (Germany). The two-inch-long wild horse from the Vogelherd cave is among the most beautiful mammoth ivory animal figure carvings. This discovery is one of the oldest known human works of art.

The richest discovery of ornaments from over 21,000 years ago was made at a grave site in Sungir, near Moscow, Russia. The three people buried there were given an unusual number of grave ornaments. The man, who was discovered in 1964, wore twenty bracelets made of mammoth ivory and a stone pendant, and more than 3,000 beads decorated his clothes. The two children found in 1969 were wearing clothes decorated with thousands of bone beads. They also wore bone breast ornaments, thin ivory bracelets, and bone thumb rings.

Decorated ivory bracelets are also known from more than 21,000 years ago. Noteworthy are the fragments of at least three ivory rings from the Magdalena cave near Gerolstein, in the Eifel region, that are decorated with a finely carved chevron pattern; one is also decorated with rows of points drilled into the material.

1.2 The Art of the Eskimo

When explorer Knud Rasmussen arrived at the harbor of Nome, Alaska, at the end of his fifth Thule Expedition in 1924, he found members of different Eskimo groups from the mainland and the surrounding islands. Rasmussen wanted to research the Eskimo lifestyle and traditions. However, since the discovery of gold in 1900 Nome had become a bustling city, so Rasmussen made the following observations in his travelogue about two years of travel through unexplored Eskimo country by sled:

Mammoths were an important source of food and raw materials for early humans. Carving signs and symbols into the teeth and bones of animals they had hunted was a feature of our ancestors' lives.

> The streets were full of Eskimos who moved around trading goods. They show the tourists curious pieces, all sorts of funny walrus tusk carvings; during the summer, this skill could earn the carver three to four hundred dollars, so he could travel back to his winter village with his most essential needs basically provided for.

These remarks indicate some essential aspects of the artistic work of that small polar population. They valued the art of carving highly. The Eskimos worked bone and teeth with great mastery. They were already making these carvings not only for their own use, but also for sale one hundred years ago.

For the Eskimo groups, ocean mammals—seals, walruses, and whales—had a dominant role in the annual pattern of their economy. They were an extremely specialized, creative hunting people whose close relationship with the animal world is expressed in many ways: not only in numerous myths and legends, but also in handcrafted and artistic works.

Next to reindeer and whale bone, the Eskimos especially valued long walrus tusks as carving material. In Alaska, these were Pacific walruses. A tusk of this animal can weigh about eleven pounds and be about three feet long.

This material has a number of properties that make it very workable. It can not only be engraved and carved, but also etched, stained, and painted. In most cases, the glossy, soft, natural tone of the bone material was retained. The addition of coloring was limited to specific sculptured details or colored highlighting of the engraved decoration.

The Eskimo knew of many different sources of raw materials for colored designs for their carvings: white was obtained from light, loamy earth; yellow and red were made from ocher earth (red also from iron oxide); and black from graphite, charcoal, or gunpowder. The latter two materials were mixed with blood to ensure better adhesion of the color. Green tones, which are found relatively rarely,

The Inuit made weapons and tools from the "raw materials" of animals not only out of pure expediency; decoration and ornamentation were an essential part of their handicraft.

were made using oxidized copper. As can be seen even recently, the Eskimos experimented with tea, coffee, ink, tar, and crude oil to create fully colored carvings. Either boiled for hours in the substance or immersed in it for days on end, the bony material undergoes a kind of tanning and takes on brownish tones.

The inhabitants of Arctic America very likely knew about iron tools long before they came in contact with whalers, traders, or white explorers. It is clear that in the period that followed they constantly strove to expand their capabilities with these implements.

In working with these bony materials, the Eskimo developed a high level of artistic handicraft. Anyone who examines these carvings will note there are significant differences in their design; though there are pieces decorated with plastic, there are others on which the carved design dominates. At the same time, these design forms express differences between the central Eskimo groups in northern Canada and those in the border zones in Alaska and Greenland. The central Eskimos decorated their carvings mostly with simple, linear ornamentation. However, from the western regions in Alaska we find, in addition to these linear engravings, many figurative, pictorial representations of animals, hunting scenes, or other events of everyday life that are usually arranged to create a picture story, if not even picture writing.

Such carved decorations can contain figurative or geometric elements such as points, circles, zigzags, waves, ridges, and other lines. Many authors have interpreted these motifs without ever coming to a convincing explanation of them.

Another step in the design of bone carvings was the creation of separate, fully rounded figures. These were primarily made in Greenland and by the Labrador Eskimo, whose animal and human figures are among the most impressive examples.

Walrus tusk is an important basic material for Eskimo carvings. A walrus provided smaller molars in addition to two large canine teeth that are also called "tusks."

Just as life itself is diverse in all its social interweavings, the work of the Eskimo carver displays a surprising variety of subjects. Here, an excellent capacity for observation—a basic precondition of the hunter's life—certainly stood the artists in good stead. A whole range of carved implements, household objects, and clothing accessories developed that was fully integrated into their original way of life.

They also designed objects that had no direct relationship to the Eskimo way of life and are therefore attributed in ethnographic collections to so-called tourist art. Nevertheless, these also deserve attention as an expression of the creativity of the Arctic peoples.

Bone was also frequently used as a basic material for hunting and work tools: bows made of bone plates (a design superior to the simpler bows made from driftwood in both range and accuracy); harpoon points and fish hooks; the so-called snow knife that was used for cutting snow blocks, but was also used for brushing off fur clothing; and the bola hurled to hunt birds testify how widely bone was used as a material. All these objects were decorated with carvings and engravings.

Clothing also included bone accessories. To prevent slipping on smooth ice, the Eskimos tied narrow strips of bone to the soles of their fur boots; these had conical cleats cut from the material on their underside. The Eskimos can also be cited as the inventors of sunglasses: to protect themselves from the reflected glare of the snowfields they used either simple wooden snow goggles with slits or eye shields elaborately decorated with applied ornamental pieces of bone made by expert carvers.

Especially charming are carvings that feature references to the highly differentiated world of the Eskimo imagination and their myths and legends, which often reflect the experiences of life and the wisdom of the people. It is not always possible to ascertain the mythical details for each individual representation. Sometimes

what might appear to be animals with human faces and seem shrouded in mystery are simple play figures used to entertain. Others, however, certainly had magical significance and were used by shamans during their performances, were hung in ceremonial houses, or were attached to boats as magical protection.

An impressive piece with such a spiritual background is a small, reclining seal that rests its slightly raised head —with forehead and eyes already portrayed as quite human-like—on human arms; in this attitude, it emphasizes the bond between man and animal. Such human-animal combinations are often encountered in the conceptual world of the Eskimo, for example, as a man-worm, and they were also depicted as combinations of various animals, such as a polar bear with a whale. These composite beings were connected to beliefs handed on in Eskimo narratives and finally recorded by researchers.

Among the original equipment of the Eskimo, a compass is just as rare as a fork. On the other hand, they knew of combs, but not primarily as a means for personal care; rather, these were used to comb out tufts of grass needed for making a warm liner for winter boots. Crochet hooks, containers for toothpicks, napkin rings, and Greek calendars (parapegma) to mark the seven-day weekly cycle were also not included among Eskimo cultural objects.

All these things became widespread after contact was made with white traders and seafarers, and especially with missionaries. The resulting demand eventually led to the emergence of a souvenir market. Among the finest pieces of early souvenir products are tobacco pipes from around the turn of the nineteenth to twentieth centuries, with carved decorations and some almost baroque molded ornamentation. The pipe the Eskimos themselves used for smoking comes from Asia; a curved wooden pipe with a funnel-shaped bowl.

Eskimo bone carving offers a handicraft and artistic image of the life of these polar peoples as it was produced—without using any other materials—up until World War II.

Whale teeth also served the Inuit as a raw material that was used for the manufacture of tools and weapons.

Men as well as whales also often lost their lives in whaling. Dramas on the high seas were favorite themes for scrimshaw engravers.

1.3 Scrimshaw among the Whalers

Whaling ships and their crews were often at sea for years on end. The whaling grounds—many thousands of miles away from home ports—were reached only after a long, grueling cruise. There was plenty of time available on board. The actual whaling took just a just a fraction of the time; most of the day was spent waiting.

As a result, many of the crew would take out a piece of whalebone or a sperm whale tooth and begin to work. The men carved and engraved scenes, ornaments, or even a little poem for their sweetheart at home into the material, inspired by the wind and the monotonous creaking of the ropes. These were the origins of the first scrimshaw that are still intertwined today with many ancient seafaring legends.

It is uncertain where the name scrimshaw comes from. The term seems related to the French (fencing) term "escrime."

THE "IVORY OF THE SEAS"

The whale was considered a true giant source of raw materials, especially in the nineteenth century. In addition to blubber, oils, fats, and precious ambergris, it also provided plenty of bone, so-called whalebone. Whale oil was needed to lubricate machinery—the machinery that set the budding century of industrialization into motion. The great cities of Europe were illuminated by lamps supplied with whale oil. Ambergris was valued as an important raw material for perfume. The ladies of the nineteenth century also wore corsets of whalebone.

Most sought after were the mighty teeth of sperm whales. They were knocked from the jaws of slain animals with axes. The highest-ranking officers on board then distributed them—more or less fairly—to the crew, who then artfully decorated the pieces. Every sailor was able to supplement his meager pay by selling his scrimshaw in ports of call. It was only the dealers who sold the "ivory of the seas" throughout the world who really became rich.

The work of the scrimshaw artist began by smoothing the wavy surface of the whale teeth. This was done using the ship carpenter's rasps and files. The men used dried skate skin for fine finishing. It was then polished using a paste of oil and ash. This gave the tooth's surface a beautiful satin sheen.

They began to work the pieces using a sail needle and sailor's knife. Line by line, prick by prick, the sailor carved and scratched into the surface. Gradually, an entire image emerged; now you had to make the engravings or carvings visible. This was achieved by rubbing the entire tooth with a paste of lampblack and oil. The pigment set firmly in the incisions of the engraving, creating a richly contrasting image.

Scrimshaw motifs were many and varied. Pictures of whales were particularly popular and represented in all conceivable variations.

THE HISTORY OF THE "ESSEX OF NANTUCKET"

In the beginning of the nineteenth century, a drama on the high seas occurred that has often been depicted in scrimshaw.

Nantucket, New England: The three-master whaler Essex set sail August 12, 1819, to hunt whales on what was expected to be a half-year voyage in the Pacific. The Essex was commanded by Captain George Pollard Junior. It was to be the last voyage of the Essex; on November 20, 1820, more than a thousand miles to the west of the Galapagos Islands, it was rammed by a giant sperm whale, making a large leak in the ship and causing it to sink.

"His aspect was terrible and indicated rage and rancor. In the second attack, the whale smashed the bow. His whole front is as hard as iron. Yes, I can compare it to nothing but the inside of a horse's hoof, on which the harpoon or lance would not make the slightest impression. For two days Captain Pollard was able to keep the ship afloat, then he gave up the wreck and set off with twenty men in three boats to reach the Marquesas Islands, which lay a good thousand nautical miles to the north-east..."

This is how Owen Case—the whaling ship's first officer—recorded the events in the ship's logbook. The crew escaped in three small boats used for hunting whales and now had a more than three thousand mile and roughly a three-month-long odyssey before them. Owen Chase commanded one of the whaleboats. They began the long journey hoping to reach the safety of the west coast of South America. The biggest problem was their very meager supplies. The men had to make do with one cup of water and a pound of hardtack per day, which was later reduced to a ration of one and a half ounces.

Owen Chase described how the men had to eat hardtack tainted with salt water, tried to ease their thirst by drinking turtle blood and their own urine, and how in desperation they devoured raw flying fish and mussels clinging to their boat. Finally, they decided to eat some dead comrades for their own survival. One man was even shot for this same reason in another whaleboat commanded by Captain Pollard.

Just before they gave up completely, the survivors in the whaleboats of Owen Chase and George Pollard were found off the coast of Chile on February 18 and 23, 1821, by the Brigg Indian and Dauphin and were taken aboard. Three crew members who voluntarily stayed behind on an island were also later saved. Overall, only eight men survived the disaster.

The whalers' life was rough and hard. Danger was a constant companion on the high seas.

The "Leviathan," in all its terrible size and appearance, which were being harpooned. The men also happily immortalized their own ships, the captain, or an incident on board. Artfully made containers, walking sticks, and all sorts of other everyday objects were also painstakingly created and are categorized as "scrimshaw." There are many exhibits in the great whaling and maritime museums of the world that document the hard life of a whaler (a visit to the German Maritime Museum in Bremerhaven is well worth it).

The sailors were often trying to escape their harsh reality by getting lost in their thoughts. Far from home, they would engrave the image of their loved ones who were waiting, looking towards the sea in the "widow's walk" on their home rooftops.

Whaling was an important industry. Large fleets sailed along the whales' migration routes in the world's oceans. Small provincial towns such as New Bedford, Nantucket, and New Bellingham grew into large port cities as collecting centers for whale "products." They were big, rich, and notorious. Ship crews came from all over the world: adventurers, Indians, slaves, the unemployed, "skilled" seafarers—anyone could be hired for the hard, dangerous job of whaling. Among these tough guys, there were also always true artists.

1.4 Scrimshaw Today

This ancient seaman's art owes its resurrection to a large extent to former US President John F. Kennedy. During his television interviews in the early 1960s, some of his old collector pieces could be seen on the screen. They were used as decorations on Kennedy's desk. The president was considered one of the greatest collectors of maritime art and scrimshaw in the US.

These television appearances inspired a real run on scrimshaw artwork. Within a short time, all the artwork had been bought up and the market was empty. International auction houses achieved top prices for old original pieces.

Foto: jfklibrary.org

John F. Kennedy was one of the most prominent and largest collectors of maritime art. Pieces from his scrimshaw collection were always on his desk in the Oval Office.

The scrimshaw boom also meant that artists and engravers became involved in this genre, creating new works. Scrimshaw also became a domestic art in Europe. Inspired by the resurgence of interest in the US, some European artists specialized in the old engraving style and developed it further.

Today, however, whale teeth and bones are no longer used for scrimshaw. Wildlife conservation no longer allows this. New materials include fossil mammoth tusks found in major deposits in Alaska and Siberia. Horn and bone of animals that are not endangered species and various plastics are also being used as basic materials.

For many years, modern scrimshaw engraving has traveled new pathways. Designs and applications have evolved and changed. Hunting art and design collectors have discovered this art. It is not surprising that today we find scrimshaw carvings on the grips and stock inlays of high-quality collector weapons. The subjects are primarily animals or wildlife scenes, but you can also find nude figures and other designs. Anyone collecting elephants, owls, or bears, for example, will also make good finds among modern scrimshaw carvings.

Scrimshaw carvings are found most commonly on knife and pistol grips. Among the very exclusive are engraved fore-end nose caps, pistol grip caps, or stock inlays on luxury hunting weapons. There are also bolo ties, brooches, and bracelets with hunting motifs. Special pieces include engraved display-art objects, in which the engraved material is shown to advantage as the object of an appropriate presentation. Ultimately, there is no limit to the imagination of a scrimshaw artist; "no limits" is the motto, especially for advanced scrimshaw carvers.

FAKESHAW: GENUINE OR NOT?

Anywhere originals can earn a lot of money fakes are usually close at hand. There are perfect replicas of original whale teeth coming from the Far East and England that initially unsettle many collectors. Inexperienced buyers sometimes realize they have spent a lot of money for a fake piece. Plastic teeth—generally referred to as "fakeshaw"— are not hand-engraved like real scrimshaw, but are cast. The manufacture of these pieces is from the late twentieth century. A first indication of a fakeshaw is often the very conspicuous, dark brown patina on the underside of the tooth, but that does not necessarily mean that every brownish, discolored tooth is a "fake."

Sometimes you can also see a badly removed casting burr or brownish, pigmented traces of milling and grinding. The tooth surface does not show the natural grain of the genuine material. Bumps and cracks in the plastic surface are often too brown colored. This "patina" does not go deep into the surface, such as in an old whale tooth with natural coloring. It can also be easily removed from the surface with a sharp blade.

Shavings and grinding dust of a fake tooth, when heated or burned, smells strongly of plastic. Shavings and grinding dust of a real tooth smell more like burnt hair or horn.

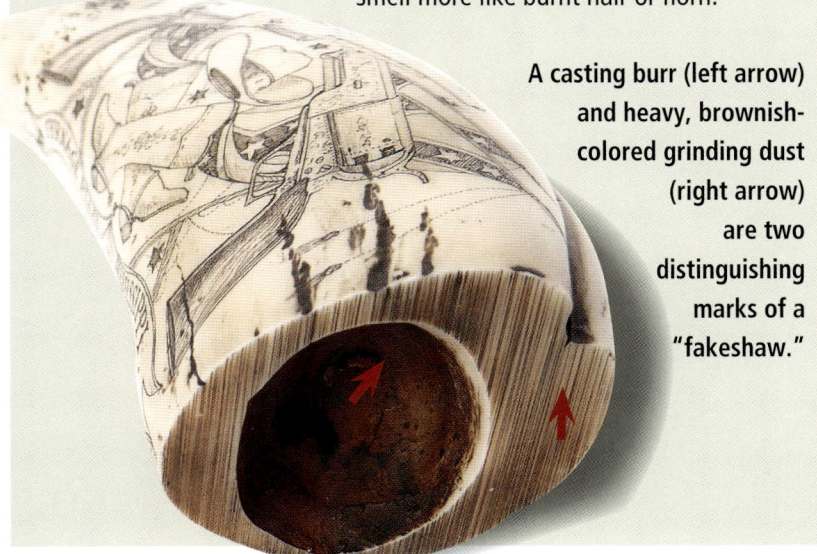

A casting burr (left arrow) and heavy, brownish-colored grinding dust (right arrow) are two distinguishing marks of a "fakeshaw."

BASIC MATERIALS

2.1 Fossilized Mammoth Ivory

Although large quantities of Ice Age tusks have been found in northern Russia and Yakutia, in the past, elephant ivory was in high demand due for its qualities and lower price. Only when the Washington Convention on Trade in Endangered Species (CITES) went into law in October 1989 to protect elephants did mammoth ivory suddenly gain new importance. Mammoth ivory is not subject to the endangered species protection agreements and may be traded freely.

Mammoth tusks can weigh up to 330 pounds and be up to thirteen feet long. Working with this fascinating material is a constant challenge and when the surface is treated, it keeps providing surprises with beautiful natural colors and structures. These make every piece a distinctive, unique object.

Mastadon tusks are closely related to mammoth ivory. The mastodon formed its own species about thirty million years ago—long before the mammoths—but also died out with the end of the last Ice Age. Mastodon ivory is a rare find and it is usually not used in scrimshaw.

Mammoth ivory is found primarily along the Siberian Arctic Ocean coast and on the sloping banks of great rivers. New discoveries are also constantly reported from the interior of Siberia and Yakutia. Russian scientists estimate there are some 700,000 tons on the Arctic coast alone. This raw material can only be exported from Russia after a scientific evaluation and with an appropriate license.

The earth—frozen up to 3,300 feet deep—has to a large extent preserved the tusks from decay. Nevertheless, the last 10,000 to

60,000 years have left their traces behind, so we can classify the material into five different grades. The two best varieties—compact and without cracks—account for only about ten percent. This quality is particularly suitable for making larger pieces, such as figures. The other grades are used to manufacture jewelry, which gets its special charm from natural discoloration due to mineral deposits. In Canada and Alaska, new finds are made mostly during gold mining. Because of their poor condition, the rare finds in Germany are not suitable for scrimshaw.

Mammoth ivory is about twenty to twenty-five percent heavier than elephant ivory. Due to its long storage in ice it has become brittle and more difficult to work. Unlike elephant ivory, the tusks are completely solid and have no hollows.

Because of its infinite variety of grain patterns and shades of color, in addition to its excellent qualities for processing, mammoth ivory is the primary basic material for modern scrimshaw carving.

2.2 Elephant Ivory

Nowadays, elephant ivory may only be processed with special permission. This involves using old stock that has been imported to Germany before the endangered species convention went into effect. Because a certificate of authenticity has to be provided in Germany since the mid-1970s, exemption is only available for proven legal imports. A respective legal record requirement for ivory (origin and delivery records, under §8 of the National Species Protection Act), which includes both removal abstraction (cutting) as well as prepared pieces, as well as the resulting waste or dust, fully documents the origin and processing of the material. There is no more mass production of ivory objects. Instead, existing inventories are used for individual work, restorations, and preservation of antique pieces.

2.3 Hippopotamus Ivory

The up to twenty-eight inch long curved canines and incisors of the hippopotamus provide the hardest ivory known. The base can reach a diameter of up to three and a half inches. A cross-section of the tusk shows a dense, fine, concentric white grain. Another characteristic is the recognizable backfilling of the inner dentin, with its ribbed, wavy structure, which is still recognizable in some fashioned art objects and makes a unique attribution of this material possible. Hippopotamus ivory appears mainly in hunting trophies from the tropical countries of Africa. Valid export and import documents are required.

DIFFERENTIATING TYPES OF IVORY

We generally refer to the tusks of proboscidea—elephants, mammoths, and mastodons—as ivory; these differ in their structure from ivory surrogates such as hippo, walrus, sperm whale or narwhal teeth and bones, or tagua nut.

Only trunked animals' ivory has the typical net-like texture. It is differentiated by the arrangement of intersecting lines. This structure—also called Schreger's lines—shows different cross hatchings that a connoisseur can detect with the naked eye.

The following data are benchmarks:

Ivory:	100-120 degrees
Mammoth:	80-90 degrees
Mastodon:	40-50 degrees

Other differences include specific gravity and occasionally the color of the material.

Ivory:	From 106 to 115½ lbs/ft3
Mammoth:	From 125 to 137 lbs/ft3

In detailed carved pieces, it is often impossible to clearly identify the structure. For such objects, there are special examination methods provided by Johannes Gutenberg University in Mainz, Germany, which has since been recognized as an official reference laboratory by the Federal Agency for Nature Conservation.

Modern spectroscopic and mass spectrometric analysis methods, as well as IR-reflection spectroscopy or laser-ablation ICP-MS, can recognize the origin of the material beyond dispute and even distinguish between African and Indian ivory.

The extremely hard enamel of hippo teeth must be ground off before carving and engraving, otherwise fine machining with steel tools is almost impossible.

2.4 Whale Tooth

Sperm whales are the largest of the toothed whales and are distributed over a vast area. The males seem to prefer the cold habitats of the North and South, while females remain with their pups in equatorial and subtropical waters. In their long, narrow lower jaw they have some twenty to twenty-five cone-shaped teeth on each side in various sizes up to six inches long. The tooth cross-section shows a thick, white hard cement layer; the interior is filled with pale yellow dentin. Both have a concentric ring pattern. There is a trade ban on sperm whale teeth.

2.5 Fossilized Walrus Tusk

The walrus has two 23 to thirty inch long, downward-pointing canine teeth in its upper jaw. The characteristic tusk structure

Sambar antler is a popular material for engraving and carving.

of the tusks is shown both in oval cross section and longitudinal section. The tusk interior has an irregular, rice-grain-like pattern. It is surrounded with an edging of ivory-colored dentin. This material is very difficult to fashion. Among the most famous walrus tusk carvings are the figures of saints and religious relief carving scenes in the Hessian State Museum in Darmstadt. Walrus tusks are sold today as a raw material or as souvenir Eskimo carvings from Alaska, Canada, and Greenland. It is required to present customs with a valid export and import authorization.

2.6 Sambar Antler

The antler of the South Asian sambar is ideal for scrimshaw carving. However, sambar antler is now no longer available because the deer is on the endangered species list, and it is increasingly difficult to obtain this material.

Because of its density, sambar antler has very few pores and little marrow. It is also barely fissured and lends itself perfectly to being ground and polished. For colors, sambar antler offers various shades from light brown shading to dark brown. Almost white colors are not uncommon.

I really enjoy carving this material, as it has a "pleasant" hardness for me; it is not too hard, nor too brittle, and after coloring, the pigment combines well with the material. Antler is completely different from plastics in this way, since plastic as a rule does not absorb pigment well.

It can be exciting to integrate the graining or sanded and rough-polished surface features into a scrimshaw carving. This is especially easy with sambar antler.

2.7 Moose Antler

Moose antler is also a very interesting material. Outside it is brownish, but is relatively light towards its center. However, one

The large surface of a moose antler shovel is perfectly suited for scrimshaw. The outer layers are usually harder and thicker. It is nevertheless important to give the uneven surface a light sanding and polishing before engraving.

Reindeer antler is a popular material for knife grips and decoration in northern cultures, and is therefore closely linked to scrimshaw.

must always reckon with more or less large "pixels" in the material. After grinding and polishing you can sometimes get a nasty surprise when coloring. The finest pores are visible only after pigment is applied. Before you use a piece for scrimshaw, test for possible lines, dots, and coloring using a sample from the same piece of antler.

I myself once skipped this test due to time constraints and found a real "gray veil" in the finished portrait engraving. This veil—viewed under a microscope—consisted of hundreds of fine pores.

2.8 Reindeer Antler

Reindeer antler, in terms of carving or engraving qualities, is very similar to moose antler. Here also you can find various shades of brown, ranging to almost pure white. You always have to take slight cracks and pores into account in the design as they constantly occur in this material.

It is interesting to sand and polish a whole antler shovel in the middle part, so that you can then work on a large area. I would personally choose designs that can be converted into line art, because it lets you rework or work over the noted "pixels" and pores much more easily, thus concealing and integrating them. You can also achieve a nice effect by coloring with sepia tones, which match perfectly with the brown tones in the outer texture.

2.9 Cattle Horn

Engraving cattle horn is a thankless task, since this material is extremely "fibrous." You cannot create any clean lines in it and the dotting technique reaches its limits. Despite this, the material is engraved and carved. I have seen wonderfully decorated drinking horns with elaborate ornamentation.

It is best to use the technique of carving and milling with fine diamond tip and flexion wave. The results are interesting, but this takes a lot of effort. I advise any engraver to preferably provide themselves with a good piece of mammoth ivory, since this will give you much more rewarding results.

There are many shades of cattle horn. For black colored scrimshaw, it is important to look for the lightest possible pieces of horn.

In general, it is Asian buffalo horn that is available and used. The horn of African buffaloes is also suitable for engraving and carving.

2:10 Buffalo Horn

The horn of the water buffalo is a fascinating material. When it is ground and polished you obtain a mirror-like, shiny, black material in which different shades of gray to green and sometimes brown hues emerge.

The special issue for scrimshaw is how you proceed: color the buffalo horn with light pigments (white). In this method called "reverse scrimshaw," the shaded sections of the design will be left blank, since they are defined by the material itself. Principally, you work from dark to light.

Buffalo horn engraved using a needle sometimes has a slight fibrous quality. Under a magnifying glass, you can often recognize a slight burr in the drawn lines. You can eventually remedy this if you polish very lightly and gently by hand, but I would only do this when necessary and where you have predominantly deeper lines.

The material also has another interesting property: the engraved patterns emerge immediately—without coloring—as light in the surface due to the fine burr produced during the carving. This makes the work a little easier, because you get to see the design before coloring. Nevertheless, coloring is essential because otherwise the contrast is too faint.

2.11 Cattle Bone

Cattle bone is quite suitable for scrimshaw carving. However, it has—like almost all bone and horn materials—the small disadvantage of inclusions and pores. Sometimes it is impossible to avoid cracks in the surface.

Cattle bone is generally colored white, but it can also be found in light cream shades. It is particularly suitable for coarse line art. Designs engraved this way enhance the character of the material. Cattle bone is now also available in sheet form, which is especially used for training purposes.

I recommend to every scrimshaw beginner, that they don't grind the engraving needle to too sharp a point when using such materials. Choose a blunter point. Bone can be carved better using line art, in my experience. The needles glide better; try it out!

2.12 Camel Bone

A material that has become increasingly popular in recent years is camel bone. Because of its greater density it has far fewer pores than cattle bone. Camel bone is now readily available from well-stocked art suppliers. Usually it is bleached white, which makes it an ideal material for high-contrast subjects.

2.13 Micarta

Micarta is composed of several layers of paper, linen, or canvas impregnated with synthetic resin and pressed. Micarta is very firm and lightweight, water resistant, stable, and unbreakable. If the individual layers are rough-polished at an angle it can show a modified grain resembling ivory. Micarta is often used for knife handles.

2:14 Bakelite

There are a number of plastics that can be used for scrimshaw. Because it has been on the market since the beginning of the twentieth century, bakelite—also called ivorine—is one of the classics. This fully synthetic plastic in colored form serves as, among other things, a substitute for gemstones, amber, and ivory.

Micarta is an excellent "training material" for scrimshaw engraving. However, it has the disadvantage that it becomes very yellowed over time and darkens.

Since synthetic resins melt when heated, bakelite can be easily detected if you pierce it with a hot needle. Take care when cleaning, because bakelite is soluble in alcohol and spirits.

2:15 Oosik

The term oosik refers to the fossilized bones of a walrus penis.

This exotic material is very popular with knife makers and engravers. I rate its handiwork qualities close to those of fossilized mammoth ivory. Since it is a bone material, however, it has the usual pores that can ultimately be seen after coloring. Oosik can be found in various shades of light brown and brown shadings.

Oosik can be obtained in various dimensions and stains. Before grinding and polishing, the pores are filled with thin liquid cyanide adhesive. Pay attention when selecting the material and find a rather light-colored oosik. This usually allows the design to show up more in contrast.

2.16 Other Materials

The seemingly endless diversity of nature offers the scrimshaw artist plenty of materials. Consider the variety of mother of pearl materials or tagua nut (also called ivory nut). Bones also offer enormous variety. If you are able to get your hands on one or another exotic piece, I can only say the proof of the pudding is in the eating.

You should always keep in mind the protection of endangered species. Always make sure that you work as much as possible with materials that can be traded and processed in accordance with the Endangered Species Act. Think in terms of nature, because we are all a part of it.

Warthog tusks offer interesting possibilities as a basis for scrimshaw. After sanding and polishing the surface this material can be readily carved and engraved.

TOOLS AND WORKING MATERIALS

3.1 Primers

In principle, a surface must first be primed before you can draw on it. Without a primer coat, you can barely make a mark on a highly polished surface such as mammoth ivory, even with a pencil. The lines are almost imperceptible and appear very blurred. Furthermore, light reflection is also a big hindrance.

One of the best and most widely used methods is to coat the surface to be carved with opaque white. It is also possible to use plasticine (plastilin) as a primer or to create a matte surface.

3.1.1 Priming with Opaque White

You can squeeze an amount of opaque white—depending on the size of the surface to be carved—directly from the tube onto the piece. Since this paste is quite thick, I use a broad hair brush dipped in water to make a thin liquid to spread on the surface of the piece. You may have to repeatedly dilute the paste with water depending on the amount used.

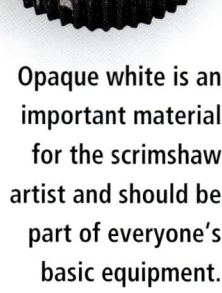

Opaque white is an important material for the scrimshaw artist and should be part of everyone's basic equipment.

SUMMARY OF PENCIL HARDNESS GRADES

Hardness	Character	Usage
9B		
8B		
7B	very soft	for artistic purposes, sketches, studies, drafts
6B		
5B		
4B		
3B		
2B	soft, dark	for freehand drawing and writing
B		
HB	medium	for writing and linear drawing
F		
H	hard	for geometric and technical drawings
2H		
3H		
4H	very hard	for detailed technical diagrams and graphs
5H		
6H		
7H	extremely hard	for special purposes, such as lithographs, cartography, xylography
8H		
9H		

The primary purpose is to achieve a wafer-thin, matte film of opaque white pigment. The thinner and smoother the surface coating, the better we can later draw nuances with a pencil. The opaque white method allows you to draw with a hard, fine pencil lead in fine and great detail. If the lines have to be corrected, I recommend you carefully roll over the lines with a kneaded eraser. This lightens the pencil lines so you can easily draw over them.

3.1.2 Priming with Plasticine

Priming with plasticine is a quick and easy method of making a matte surface. This method is best suited for preliminary work that does not have to be extremely detailed, because the pencil line does not show up as clearly on a matted with plasticine surface as on a surface primed with opaque white.

For this, I take a small piece of plasticine modeling clay and roll it over the working surface with my fingers. The back-and-forth movement leaves a slight matte abrasion on the highly polished surface of the piece. Now you can draw on the prepared surface.

If pencil marks have to be corrected, you only have to dab the incorrectly drawn portion with plasticine. The pencil line will quickly fade until it disappears almost completely. Now you can draw over the lines again.

You can copy the contours of a picture on tracing paper and then transfer them to the piece's surface.

A good range of engraving needles is essential
for scrimshaw. Every collection should include
various cutting edges and points. The steel's
hardness and elasticity are important criteria
for selecting your needles.

3.2 Pencils

Pencils are usually used for sketching and tracing out the design. Experience has shown that mechanical pencils are best suited for this work. The basic rule is: the finer the detail in the sketched lines and patterns, the harder the pencil lead.

Mechanical pencils are available in 0.3, 0.5, and 0.7 mm lead diameter. To emphasize sketched contour lines, HB 0.5 mm lines are recommended. For the finest guidelines in a design a 6H 0.3 mm makes sense. For rough guidelines that only represent indications of the design flow you can also use a normal pencil with an HB lead.

3.3 Transfer Materials

3.3.1 Tracing Paper

Tracing paper is available in different types and weights. You can buy it in single sheets, blocks, and rolls. I recommend making sure the paper weight is neither too thick nor thin. Too thin paper can tear easily. Be sure when you buy it that the paper is also very transparent. A little tip: cut the paper into small pieces corresponding approximately to the dimensions of the piece.

3.3.2 Blueprint Paper

Blueprint paper—also called carbon paper—was used to copy documents before the advent of copiers, PCs, and printers. This very thin, special paper is an abrasion-resistant semi-gloss on one side with a special color layer on the other.

You can lay the color-coated surface on a sheet of white paper with a printed sheet on top. If you trace over the lines of the printed sheet with a pencil, the corresponding lines are imprinted

Gravers come in all kinds of types and styles. The important thing is that the graver handle (the grip) fits comfortably in your hand.

on the white sheets beneath. Unfortunately, this paper is now very difficult to obtain, since it is rarely used anymore.

3.4 Needles

A scrimshaw carver's most important tool is their engraving needle. There is no magic recipe for how a scrimshaw needle should look. The carver has to determine for themselves which needle works best. The form and nature of the engraving stylus is ultimately dependent on the subject and pattern you are about to engrave.

Steel needles, scribers, and lithographic needles are, in principle, all suitable for scrimshaw. An alternative is a special diamond-tipped needle. From my experience, steel needles are best suited, since you can change the cutting angle at any time (by regrinding).

It makes sense to have a selection of needles in your toolbox. Get needles with different cutting angles made of different steels. I will go into more detail on preparing and grinding engraving needles later on.

3.5 Gravers

A variety of hand gravers are important tools for advanced scrimshaw carvers. Using these tools requires some experience and sureness.

A classic hand graver consists of the graver handle (grip) and the actual graver. Both are often sold separately. The handle is usually made of wood, but can also be made of aluminum or plastic. I prefer traditional wooden handles, simply because they fit best in your hand and, in contrast to plastic handles, will absorb sweat when you are working and not slip. Handles can also be obtained in various forms. The thickness and length should depend on the carver's own hand and the type of engraving technique. Here, too, experience plays an important role when engraving.

For a very fine stipple work and gossamer lines I recommend a light, very slim, and especially handy grip. For chiseling out backgrounds and very broad, deep lines that require a lot of pressure, a thicker handle with a solid knob works better. Experience will show any scrimshaw engraver the way over time.

The actual graver is classified in different types. The most important types that can also be used for scrimshaw are the onglette graver, round-end graver, flat-edge graver, square graver, and knife graver.

Usually, the engraver has to assemble the metal graver and handle. Drilling a hole in the handle using a small thin wood drill is recommended; set it in the middle, vertical to the position where the graver will be anchored in the handle.

MOUNTING THE GRAVER

The so-called tang is ground to a point. Pay attention here that the steel does not become too hot and discolored (danger of breaking).

A fine, pre-bored hole in the graver handle (wooden grip) makes it easier to hammer in the graver later.

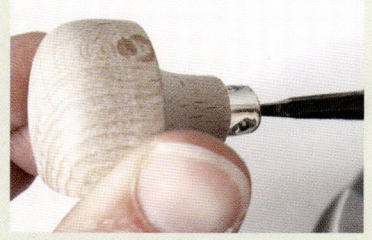

The graver handle is positioned in alignment to the tapered tang of the metal graver.

The graver, clamped in a vise, is now lightly hammered together with the handle.

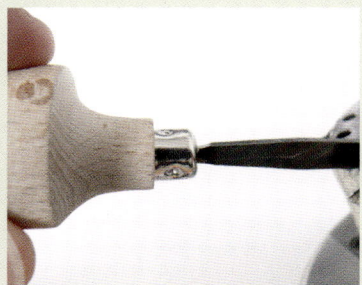

The metal graver should now be fastened tightly with the wooden handle.

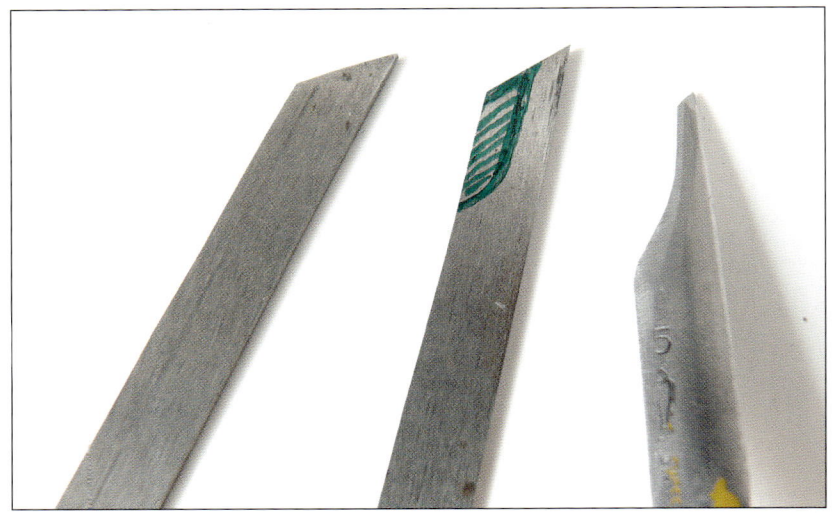

Any excess material should be sanded away from the graver blank to get a good view of the graver point. This makes it easier to re-grind the tip ("cap") later.

The back section of the graver (called the tang) is now carefully sanded with rounded edges to form a nail-like point. It is important not to let this part of the graver, which will later be hammered into the wooden handle, be tarnished blue or yellow during grinding. Otherwise, the steel loses its hardness. Keep cooling the graver in cold water (preferably in a water tank right next to the grinder).

The graver is now clamped in a vise so that the tang is perpendicular in the plumb and projects upwards about ¾ to 1¼ inches out of the vise. Now, the drilled end of the wooden handle is positioned perpendicular to the pointed tang with the left hand and hammered onto it with a plastic hammer, until the graver tang has been bored deep into the wooden handle. Hammer carefully, because the wooden handle may crack if it is hit too hard.

Now the graver is a single piece, but you still cannot use to really carve. Using the grinding disk, its length is ground off the front part of the graver. This is necessary so that the graver cap can be

GRINDING THE GRAVER

Grind off material from the back of the graver point to get a better view of the graver point.

Grind the left side of the graver to the desired radius or angle.

The right side is now adjusted to the left, to create a straight cutting edge.

It is important to grind the tip at about a 45-degree angle at the end of the grinding process.

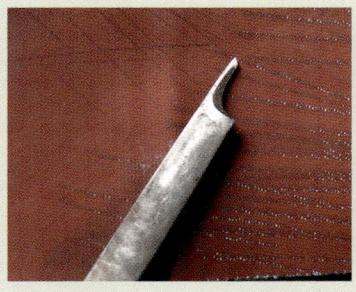

The graver's sides are ground down using fine emery cloth (1200).

Finally, the tip is sanded down.

ground more easily and especially to get a better view of the cutting section.

Then you can polish the cutting edge. If the cutting edge remained straight, the graver would bore directly into the material. You cannot draw a good line with it. It is important to give the graver a cutting angle of a few degrees. This is best done with a commercial oil grindstone. For fine polishing, 600 and 1200 grit sandpaper is particularly good, which you can glue to a flat, solid surface (using spray adhesive). For backing, a solid metal plate works particularly well or a coated plastic work surface.

The last step is grinding the point of the graver. This polish determines how the graver will handle during carving. The ideal is a 45-degree angle. This angle can also be carefully pre-ground on a grinder. Constant cooling in water is again important so as not to overheat the metal. A graver cutting section that becomes blue will quickly break.

After the rough grinding comes polishing on the grinding stone and again finishing with sandpaper. The last sanding should not be done in a crosswise direction, but along the edge. Finally, push the graver point carefully into a soft block of wood to prevent any possible fine burr.

Now comes the crucial question: can the graver carve or not? You can recognize an engraver or hand graver user by his roughened thumb nails. To make a trial carving, slide the graver point carefully over your thumbnail. A sharp graver does not slide over the nail, but "bites" it tightly. This means the graver can carve.

Finally, a word about the steel quality for gravers: HSS gravers are the best. They are notable for their specially good capability to hold an edge and elasticity. For soft materials this aspect is not essential. However, if you work with harder materials this is very important, because you do not have to re-grind the graver point as often. When you use a graver for long periods and frequently, it is recommended to wrap the entire metal area except the point with several rows of tape (masking tape), since otherwise the metal edges will press uncomfortably into your fingers.

3.6 Steel Punch and Engraving Hammer

Metal punches are a tool for the advanced scrimshaw engraver. They are used to strike different patterns into the material's surface. The center punch, matting punch, beading punch, concave punch, and dotting or graining punch are most suitable for this engraving technique.

Some manufacturers offer metal punches. Another possibility is making punches yourself. Buying ready-made punches and if necessary grinding them more makes the most sense to me. Again, the rule is to obtain the best available material (HSS).

A good assortment of steel punches accumulates over the years and facilitates future work.

Engraving punches are available in a wide variety of punch patterns, lengths, and diameters. I don't think it is necessary to provide yourself with the full range of punches. What is important is to have one or two center punches with different angles in your toolbox. Matting punches are also very useful; their different diamond patterns are well suited to structure and matte different backgrounds.

You need an engraving hammer with an engraving punch. Here too, my view is that a punching or engraving hammer bought in a specialty shop will fulfill your requirements. A lighter, smaller hammer and a slightly heavier, larger one are sufficient. If you have the opportunity, try out several hammers. What is important is that the hammer fits your hand well.

3.7 Magnifiers and Microscopes

Anyone wanting to make scrimshaw engravings has to take magnifiers and microscopes into account. They should at least have a good table magnifying glass in their toolbox. It makes sense to have at least six times magnification. A fixed table magnifier is ideal, set in an appropriate bracket. When selecting a magnifying glass, be sure you pay attention to quality and brand-name products. Nothing can be more annoying while you are working than a magnifier table stand that keeps shaking. Seek advice from a specialist dealer or optician. Test the magnifying glass of your choice.

Another possibility is to use a headband magnifier. However, headband magnifiers begin to be a bother after working for a few hours.

A practical solution is to occasionally use a so-called linen tester. These small hand magnifiers are used in the printing industry to detect fine details in printed material. I like to use these magnifiers in between; for example, for very curved surfaces. A small disadvantage is that you constantly need to use one hand to hold the magnifying glass.

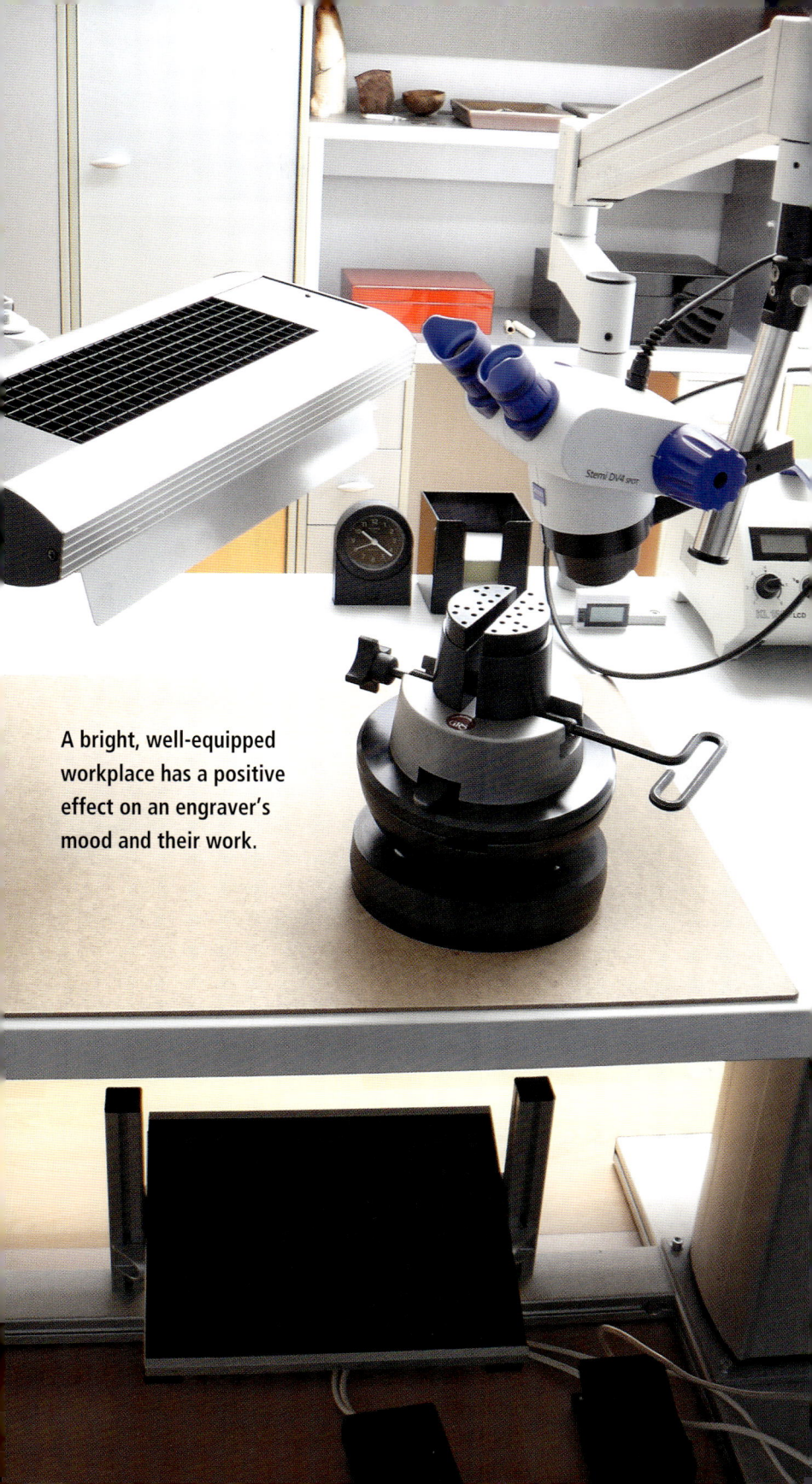

A bright, well-equipped workplace has a positive effect on an engraver's mood and their work.

For professional scrimshaw jobs a microscope is essential. Again, you should not skimp on quality. You only have one pair of eyes! Personally, I use a Zeiss Stemi brand stereo microscope with appropriate lighting apparatus and a special holder. After a few hours of hard work you can clearly tell the difference between good and faulty equipment.

3.8 Lamps and Lighting

Another very important aspect of your equipment is lighting in the workplace. A workplace with plenty of natural light is ideal. Indirect light is preferred here, so that the sun does not shine directly on your piece. Too much direct sunlight will reflect too much and does not do your eyes any good.

Now to the technical lighting: in any situation, use cold light lamps. Mounting fluorescent lights on the ceiling right over your workplace is optimal. Additionally, at least one, and preferably two or three light sources are useful on your work surface. These should not be rigidly mounted, so you can move and align them as desired. This has to do with reflections on the piece. I will go into this later.

3.9 Sanding

Polishing horn and bone materials requires a lot of care because we are dealing with natural materials, some of them thousands of years old. I work with sandpaper in different grits of 240, 400, and 600 to 1200. The fastest way is to first work with a belt sander (with suction, because the sanded dust can be harmful), then keep working in a series of steps, up to the 1200 paper. I recommend—especially for flat surfaces—after using 1200 paper to rub the surface with 00/00 steel wool, which can be soaked with some grinding oil.

Specialty shops offer a good selection of sanding materials.

After sanding, thorough cleaning of the ground surface is called for, ideally with compressed air or a soft brush made of animal hair. The surface must be clean before being polished.

3.10 Polishing

The foundation of any scrimshaw engraving is a perfectly prepared surface, including a clean polish. There are basically two ways to polish: by hand or, alternatively, polishing with the appropriate equipment.

Let's start with hand polishing: use a very soft cotton cloth. Blended fabrics are less suitable because they can slightly abrade the material. For example, you will ultimately see this on mammoth ivory under magnification when you are carving. Also, make sure that the cotton is clean and does not contain any dust particles or metal shavings from steel wool.

Several products can be used as polishing agents for hand polishing. I have had very good experience with acrylic and plastic polishing pastes. Various paint polishing pastes and car finish polishes also work well.

Before the actual polishing, the material surface should again be thoroughly cleaned with acetone to remove any grease and fine sanding or metal particles. Then take some polishing paste on the cotton cloth and rub in even strokes across the working surface— it is best to first run lengthwise and then crosswise.

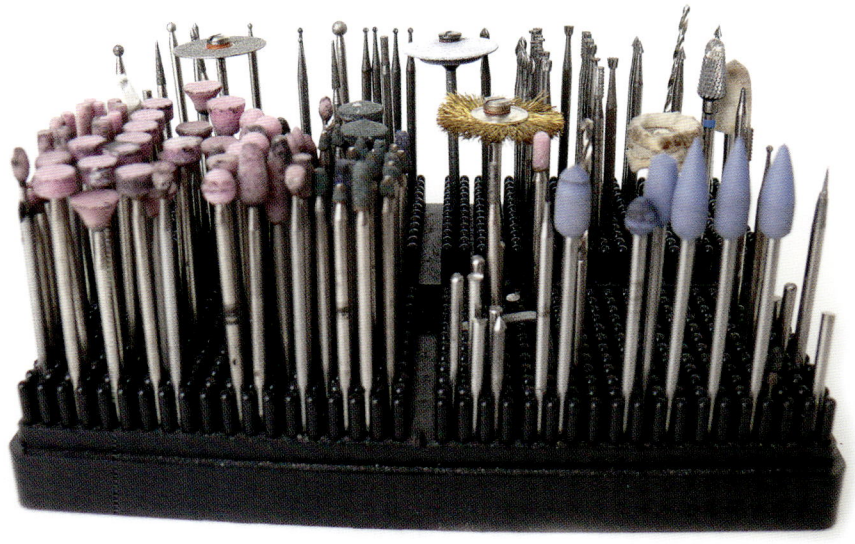

Various grinders, milling cutters, and polishing tools for micro motor-driven hand pieces (Dremel brand) make your work considerably easier.

If you have done your pre-grinding cleanly enough, you should now get a high gloss. Depending on the size and nature of the material, this step may take several minutes or longer. Finally, the residues of polish should be removed with a clean, soft cotton cloth. Well-saturated jewelry polishing cloths work very well.

Hand polishing is particularly suitable for smaller objects. For beginners, I recommend this method for the sole reason that you do not need to use machinery. I also think it is fun to see how the material changes under your own hands and begins to shine.

For a machine polish you must have a polishing machine. Different types of cloth and material discs can be attached to these machines. There are different pastes used for polishing. I use mainly commercial polishing waxes available in block form.

The polishing wax is applied to the material on the rotating disc. Hold the wax against the disc using light pressure. This way, the polishing wax is uniformly absorbed by the disc. It is important to wear eye protection when working with a polishing machine.

Now bring the piece—carefully held in both hands—up to the rotating polishing disc and move it, using gentle pressure, back and forth against the wheel. Depending on the piece's size and the material you may have to reapply polishing wax to the disc during polishing.

When using this polishing method, make sure the piece you are working on does not get too hot, since that can quickly lead to the formation of stress cracks. Also make sure you do not "burn" the material. This can happen when you polish any one area too long with too much pressure.

At the end of the polishing process clean off all residues of polish with a clean, soft cotton cloth, then check the work.

I again hold the work under a cold light source. This allows you to detect uneven surfaces or matte, unpolished clean areas easily.

3.11 Clamping Tools

Instead of holding the piece with your bare hand, it is recommended to clamp it in an appropriate device. One way to do this is to use one of the many vises available in hardware stores. Precision mechanical vises—set on a ball joint and able to turn and swivel in all directions—usually have jaws with protective coating for delicate pieces. They are easy to mount on all types of workplaces. This allows you to attach a piece securely and turn it in the optimal position needed.

When purchasing an engraving block, you should not economize on quality. Pay attention to sound workmanship and accessories.

A tip: Cut out small rectangles of thick cowhide and attach them with double-sided tape to the jaws as additional protection against pressure points.

Anyone who wants to do regular scrimshaw should consider purchasing a so-called engraving block or ball vise. An engraving block is essentially a solid steel ball that can revolve on its inner ball bearing. The ball is mounted in a leather or plastic ring so that it can be swiveled in any direction. This gives you optimal ability to clamp the piece between the jaws set on the ball.

I myself have been using engraving blocks for over twenty years. The time advantage is enormous. You can revolve or turn the piece very rapidly in any position necessary. Nothing will shake or vibrate while you are working.

This handmade engraving block is mounted on a ball bearing and can be turned especially easily. This is an advantage when engraving smaller curves or radii.

3.12 Coloring

Coloring is an important issue. Most of the time India ink is used in scrimshaw. Also popular are oil paints, acrylics, lino printing inks, and printing inks. The choice of pigment depends on the type of engraving and the artist. The pigment can be either a thin fluid like the various India inks, but can also be a thicker paste.

When selecting the pigment, it is also important to consider what effect you want to achieve. There are pigments that are more transparent, while others cover better. Transparent pigments are not completely opaque; the already colored layers will gleam through the newly applied layers of pigment. I like to use this effect if the basic material I am carving has a natural brown color and I am using sepia colors (brown tones) and traditional black. This way, I achieve shadings between dark brown and black.

With the frequent application of "glazed" black you can create softer transitions, because something of the sepia brown will still shimmer through and the color gradually merges into the black.

Glazed pigments usually dry somewhat more slowly. When using this coloring process, you should reckon on increased time for intermediate drying.

When I structure a scrimshaw work so that I work over my design in different "layers" then the use of glazing immediately suggests itself. In high-contrast designs, very opaque pigments that cover extremely well are appropriate. Pasty and "mushy" pigments usually cover better than thin, liquid ones. Also make sure the pigment you choose is not too oily. From my experience, oily pigments do not adhere well and dry very slowly.

It is worth a visit to a specialty art supply store. Select some pigments that you can test later on sample pieces.

Different shades of pasty consistency and similar products (for example, acrylic paints or printing inks) can be mixed together well. Black and light beige can be mixed into interesting brown and sepia tones.

3.12.1 Calligraphy Ink

This is a very thick, paste-like India ink. When dry, it is light-fast and waterproof. If you combine it with other India inks, beautiful matte-gloss effects can be achieved.

3.12.2 China Ink

This black drawing ink is made of glue and lampblack or carbon black. This composition gives it great depth of tone. Chinese ink is waterproof, light-fast, high-yielding, and flows well. When it is applied undiluted the ink is jet black. You can achieve shadings of gray by diluting it and applying with a brush.

3.12.3 Litho Ink

This well-proven ink is waxy, thick, and creamy. Thanks to its very finely ground consistency it is easy to work with. It can be rubbed into engraved lines very readily with a cotton swab or cotton cloth. Before starting work let the ink soften—depending on the desired consistency—by adding a small amount of warm water. This way you can create a specific "mixture," depending on the line depth and design.

3.12.4 India Ink

India ink is versatile. Undiluted, the ink is opaque. It can be diluted well with water and is ideally suited for partial inking using a brush.

3.12.5 Shellac Ink

The high proportion of ink combined with shellac gives these inks a special color brilliance and unique luminosity. When applied with a brush they produce—depending on the amount used—a satiny to a luster finish. They dry quickly and are very water resistant. Shellac ink can also be combined with acrylic or other inks.

In experimenting mixing inks, I have thickened shellac ink with black pigments. The resulting mixture can be rubbed into engraved patterns with excellent results.

3.12.6 Airbrush Pigments

Airbrush pigments are finely pigmented and very fade-resistant. With a water-soluble acrylic binder they dry quickly and are then waterproof.

Applied in thin layers they may be used as a glaze. As you add more and more layers airbrush pigment becomes opaque. Normally, this pigment is used undiluted. However, you can dilute it with up to two parts water without any problem.

3.12.7 Lino Printing Ink

Lino printing inks are ideal for coloring engraved designs that you are coloring over several times, or "glazing." The ink can be diluted with appropriate glaze mediums. The disadvantage of diluted lino ink is its long drying time. Because these inks remain water soluble, they are not suitable for scrimshaw carvings on knife handles and other objects that are often touched.

Cotton swabs saturated with thinner can be used almost like a brush to apply coloring (in this picture, lino printing ink). For smaller surfaces and transitions you can also use a fine hair brush.

There is a wide selection of acrylic pigments, so it is a good idea to try different pigments from different manufacturers. Mixing and diluting the pigments to test them is also advisable. Just relax and enjoy experimenting. It is always amazing what new effects can be achieved this way.

3.12.8 Acrylic Pigment

The dried pigment layer is elastically hard, perfectly adherent, and resistant to aging. Acrylic pigment is a highly concentrated paste and can be thinned with water. The disadvantage is that it dries very quickly, so you have to work fast.

3.12.9 Oil Pigments

High-quality oil pigments have very good light resistance. Depending on the addition of mediums and drying accelerators, the consistency ranges from a thin liquid to pasty. The advantage is that you can work in various layers of glazing. The disadvantages are the lower abrasion quality and, depending on the mixture, a long drying time.

3.12.10 Printing Ink

Printing inks have a high pigment content and an excellent covering capability. Depending on viscosity and the pigment used, printing inks can be smeared more or less well. Some black tones, because of their high viscosity, are difficult to wipe. To make them easier to wipe in you can add some linseed oil to the ink before it is rubbed into the engraved lines. If the ink is too runny, you can thicken it by adding transparent white.

After the ink is dry it has good abrasion resistance, but the drying process can take up to two weeks.

Printing inks are available in different colors that can be mixed to create new tones. You can create interesting sepia tones from red and black that can be used for coloring designs on brown basic materials. You can achieve very good transitions on polished, brownish mammoth ivory in dotted engraving designs with such pigment mixtures.

WORKING TECHNIQUES

4.1 Selecting the Right Subject

Selecting your subject is a very complex issue. Which theme suits which object depends on many factors, not least being the artist's or client's own taste. You should also observe some basic rules:

1. The scrimshaw engraving should always be adapted to the character of the object to be carved. The handle of a Bowie knife, for example, works perfectly for bears, Indians, or moose. An engraved scene from the Thirty Years' War would be out of place here.

2. Match all the effort it will require to carve the scrimshaw appropriately with the value of the object itself. It would be a shame to invest hundreds of hours of engraving work when the knife that you engrave is worth only twenty dollars.

3. Design a draft for your subject so that it fits the shape of the object. The object and scrimshaw should form a "unit" and ideally complement each other.

4. If the surface of your material has a particularly nice grain, such as mammoth ivory, then try to choose a subject that can be incorporated into the grain.

5. Less can be more: For some objects, such as a knife with a very lively damascene pattern, you should consider whether it would be too much to decorate the handle with a scrimshaw engraving. It could quickly become " overdone."

6. Engrave subjects that suit you. Anyone who particularly likes to create ornaments and has already done intensive work in this area should take advantage of this capability. You will

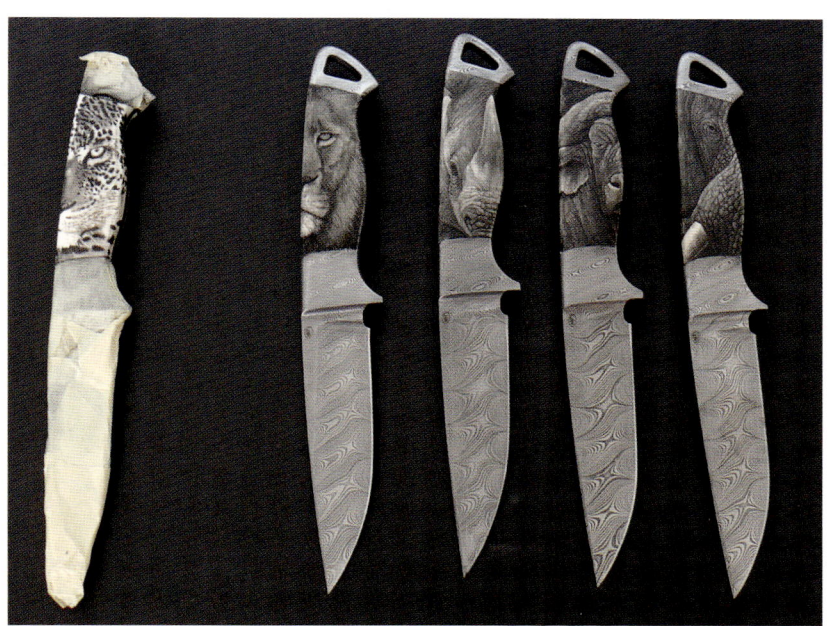

Working designs into surfaces and objects requires a lot of planning and instinctive feeling. For a set of knives, the individual designs should be selected to complement each other.

certainly see this in the quality of the work. You should not even consider things that in the truest sense of the word go "against the grain."

7. Take the object to be engraved into your hands often. Place it somewhere where you will see it "in passing" several times a day. Cast a glance at it every now and then. You will be astonished by the "flashes of thought" and ideas that will spontaneously come to you on your choice of subject.

8. Always remember when you choose your subject that you also have to execute the design and engraving technically. Think through the design piece by piece and consider what techniques you can use to execute the individual passages.

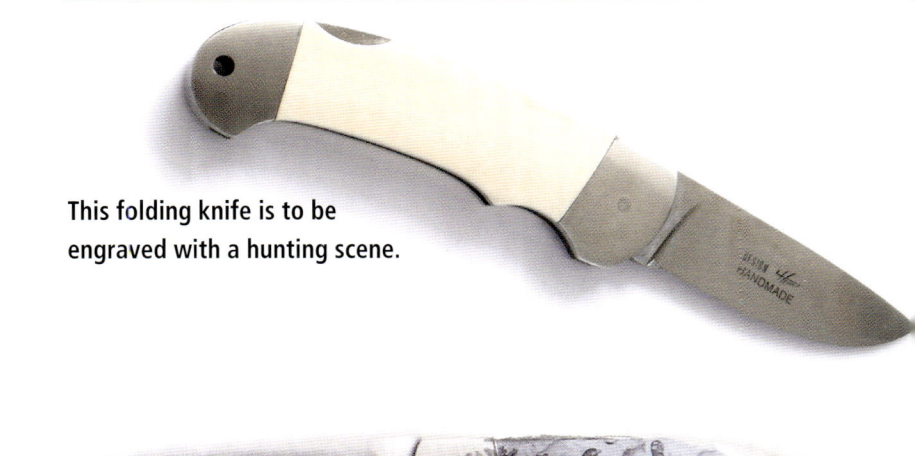

This folding knife is to be engraved with a hunting scene.

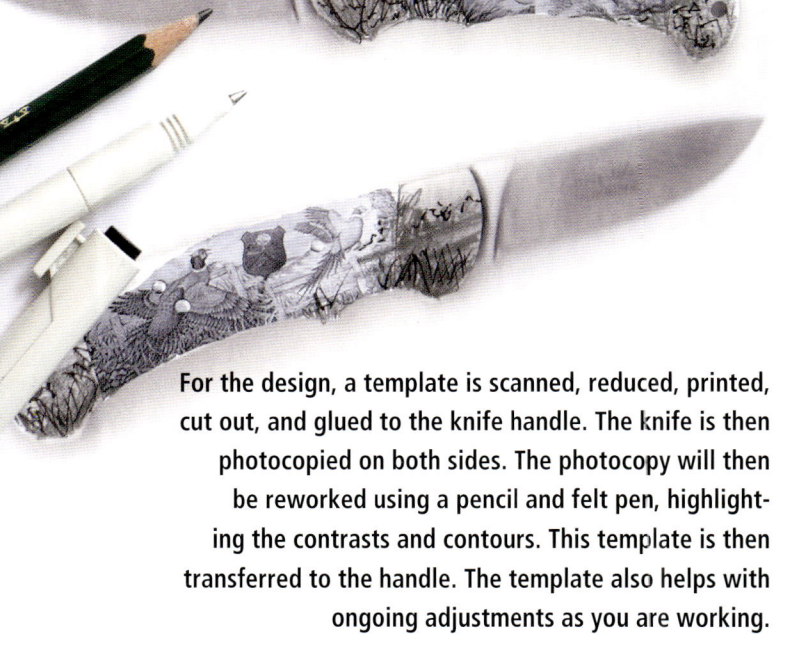

For the design, a template is scanned, reduced, printed, cut out, and glued to the knife handle. The knife is then photocopied on both sides. The photocopy will then be reworked using a pencil and felt pen, highlighting the contrasts and contours. This template is then transferred to the handle. The template also helps with ongoing adjustments as you are working.

4.2 Preparing a Design

There are many methods for preparing a design. Ultimately, the type of preparation depends on the engraver's artistic skills. Here, I want to describe an established method based on an example. We are preparing this design for a scrimshaw engraving of a knife handle.

Initially, we need the contours of the knife handle, ideally enlarged. I photocopy the knife for that purpose, or I can scan it. Then I enlarge the copy in the graphics program on my PC and print it the appropriate enlargement.

Now I have the scale enlargement and can begin to apply the subject design. In my designs, I try from the outset to emphasize the edge and contour lines. Sometimes I add copies of photos that I afterwards supplement and rework with pencil lines. This way, I sometimes create "collages" based on my ideas.

It is important for the beginner to create the most precise defined design right from the start, since that significantly facilitates your scrimshaw engraving later on.

4.3 Testing the Material

Before you start recording and engraving, you should test the material to be engraved. For a knife handle, it would be ideal to use a roughly polished scrap piece from the handle material. Mammoth ivory is not always the same mammoth ivory. Each material reacts differently. Sometimes there is graining and a fiber orientation you have to pay attention to. Materials may have cavities and a "spongy" surface. Even if a polished cattle bone looks smooth, it is still not dense enough to be engraved, not by a long shot. Engraved lines can break or fray the surface.

You should also color the material even before engraving, as a test. This lets you determine whether the material surface absorbs the pigment or not. Sample coloring your initial engraving is also useful. Not every material absorbs pigment the same way. Some surfaces require deeper engraving, while others absorb pigment well in just shallow cuttings. Over time you will develop a feel for this based on experience.

4.4 Tracing and Transferring Your Subject

There are various methods to transfer a design to a piece. I will discuss the most common ways below.

4.4.1 "Stippling" Method

After you have worked out your design, enlarge it using a copy machine or PC (scanned) to the size you will use to engrave it later. Print or copy the design on paper as thin as possible and cut the piece of paper with scissors or a cutter to the appropriate size.

For the next step, spray the back of the paper with a spray adhesive. Be careful not to use too much glue. Fix the design on the piece so that it is firmly attached.

Now you need the sharpest possible needle polished extremely thin. Carefully push the contours and the important guide lines

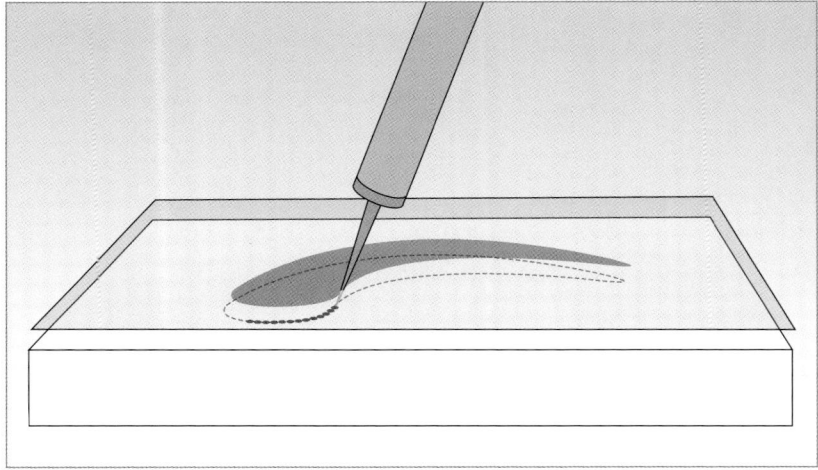

A transparency or tracing paper with the transferred design template is then placed and positioned on the piece. Puncture the contours of the subject design using a sharp needle. After removing the transparency, the punctured dots can be seen on the polished surface of the material.

through the paper, point by point. Make the dots very close together. This calls for a bit of practice—it is best to try if beforehand on a "test piece"—and also a magnifying glass or a microscope.

Then carefully pull the paper away. Glue and paper residue can be easily removed with a little thinner. Now your design should be visible in the form of contour lines screened in small dots on the surface of the material. The result depends on how carefully you have done the transfer. Now you can test color the surface. After this your design should finally be easily visible.

This stippling method is especially suited for dense, highly polished surfaces. It works less well on very porous material surfaces, since it is difficult to assess through the paper how the needle "pricks" into the material.

4.4.2 Stencil Method

Anyone who has ever tried to draw on a highly polished mammoth ivory surface will have quickly realized that this is almost impossible. It is hard to see the pencil line because of the light reflections. Therefore, we coat the surface initially with opaque white.

Simply squeeze a drop of opaque white from the tube onto the surface, then take a thicker hair brush you have moistened with water and brush a fine film of opaque white evenly over the entire engraving surface. A neat distribution of the layer is important. The more even it is, the easier it is to transfer the design afterwards. The opaque white dries within a few minutes. Make sure that it is really dry!

Now take your design in hand. It is important to have the design in 1:1 relation to the size you will actually execute. Make sure it fits to the millimeter! Place a piece of tracing paper over the subject design. The tracing paper should be easily "transparent" and not too thick.

The rubbings from plasticine modeling clay matte the polished surface so that you can sketch on it with a pencil. You can achieve an even better priming effect by applying opaque white. Sketching is then nearly as easy as on paper.

The best way to fix the tracing paper over your design is by the two upper corners. Make sure that it completely covers the whole design. It should extend over the edge a little.

Now trace the contours and individual guide lines of your design step by step on the tracing paper. To do this, use a very hard pencil with 0.3 mm lead. A hard lead allows you to do fine work. Sharpen the pencil lead as often as possible. It is a very good idea to have a worn piece of 1200 grit sandpaper that you can use to hone the lead perfectly.

The more guide lines you include on the transparency, the easier it will make it later to execute the engraving. In the next step, turn over the tracing paper with the fully sketched-out guide

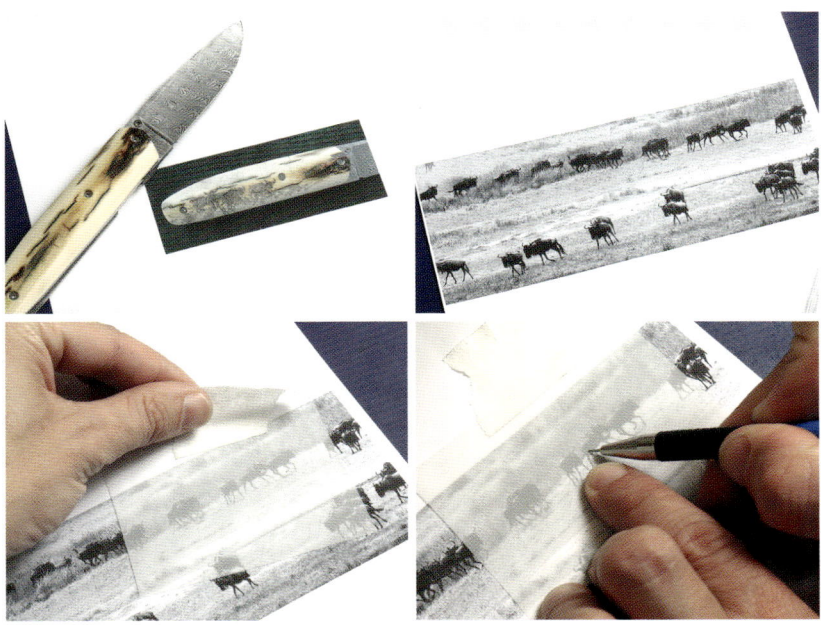

The contours of the design are transferred to tracing paper with a pencil. Fix this paper well with tape so it cannot slip.

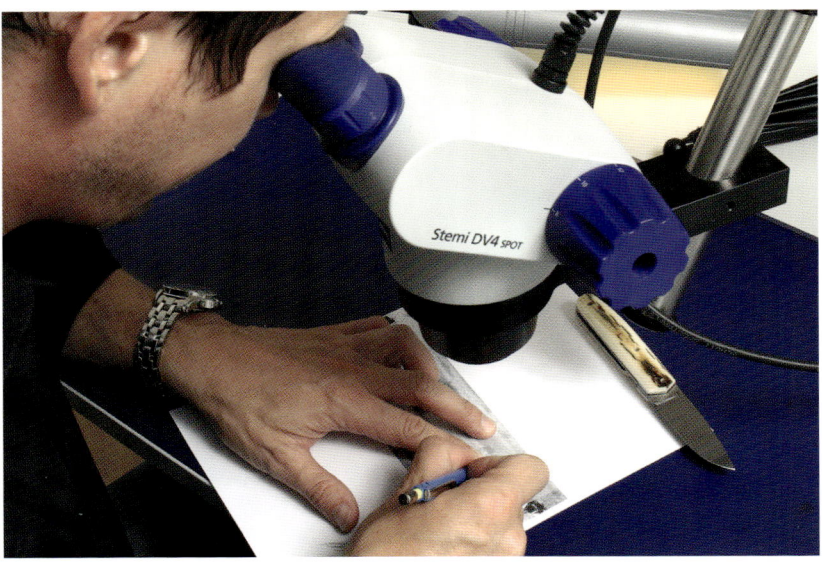

For fine contours, sketch them out under a magnifying glass or microscope.

lines. Retrace all the lines again on the back—thus mirror-inverted—side. Do not forget any of the lines; here again, please be very careful and keep rechecking.

Now you can fasten this "contour template" on the piece. Adjust the tracing paper carefully. It is really important that everything is in the correct place and not at an angle or off-center. Fasten your template to the edge areas with tape. Masking tape is recommended because it holds well and leaves no adhesive residue. Fasten the template in such a way that you can fold it up from one side, so that you can later check whether the transfer process has worked.

Now comes the key point in making the transfer: Using a blunt steel needle, rub gently over the tracing paper template. I recommend you proceed line-by-line to achieve a clean result. It is important that the needle has a really well-rounded tip, since otherwise you can tear the tracing paper and in some circumstances damage the material surface underneath. Alternatively, you can also use a blunt, hard pencil. From time to time lift up the tracing paper and carefully check the results.

The subject design's contours should now be visible on the opaque white-coated surface. It has been replicated. If the transparency slipped despite being fastened, repeat the process again from the beginning. Opaque white can be easily removed with a damp cloth.

4.5 Tracing

In general, the traced contour lines are not quite sufficient for you to begin engraving. I draw over all the lines with a hard and fine pencil (under a magnifying glass or a microscope). The more finely and in detail you sketch the lines and structures, the easier it is later to execute the scrimshaw engraving. You can even create the first shading in the tracing phase to improve your feel for the design and its subsequent execution.

Redraw the contours on the underside of the paper. Select a very hard pencil lead, ideally 0.3 mm lead size. Enough graphite must be applied to make it possible to transfer the design onto the handle material.

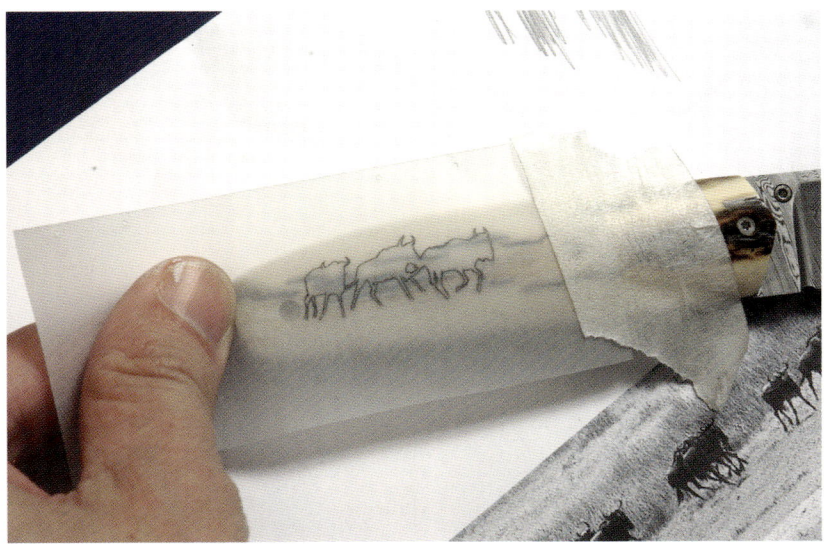

Now the finished template is positioned on the piece and fastened with tape.

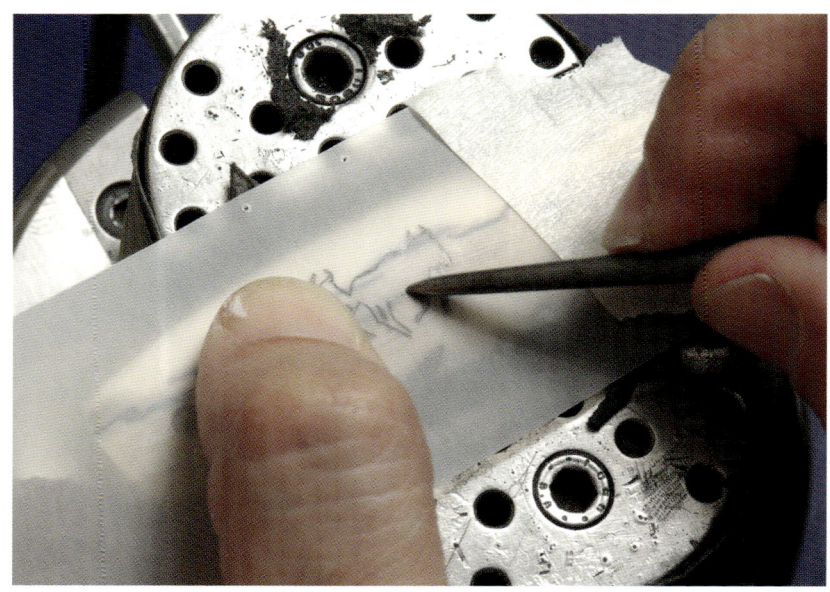

When you rub over the pencil lines drawn on the underside of the tracing paper with a blunt metal needle, they are rubbed through …

… onto the opaque white-covered surface of the material. Keep checking the contours have transferred cleanly.

Now prepare a well-sharpened lead pencil that you have honed on fine sandpaper using a twisting motion.

The lines replicated by rubbing over the graphite will be reworked using a pencil and gone over finely.

4.6 Engraving the Contours

Now the actual engraving begins. Up until now it has been crucial to sketch cleanly. The more accurately the work has been carried out so far, the more exact the engraved contours will be.

In general, contour lines can also be "contour dots." Depending on the subject, you should consider whether it makes more sense to engrave a line or whether finely grid dots are more suitable.

Here is an example: If you want to engrave the outer contours of a hairy grizzly bear, it makes more sense to engrave this with a rather blunt needle. If you had cloud formations in the background of said grizzly bear, you would outline these with finely strung together dots and a fine, sharp needle.

This creates the most realistic representation possible. Now you can shape the entire scene in traditional linework. Here you work only with hatching and lines for the cloud area. However, if you plan to present the whole picture—including the hairy coat—using the finest stipple technique, you would also work with more or less fine dots in engraving the contours.

The choice of contour needle and its cut also depends on the method of execution. For example, if I engrave large work areas focusing on fur structures and lines, I usually choose a thicker needle with a slightly blunter angle. I prefer finer needles when I am using a pure stippling technique.

Now we come to the work steps: Using a magnifying glass or microscope, you start—with gentle pressure, line for line and point by point—to work. Under magnification you can see a slight ridge thrown up by the material and the opaque white. This is important, because in a more complex design you can easily lose track of which lines are already pre-engraved and which are not.

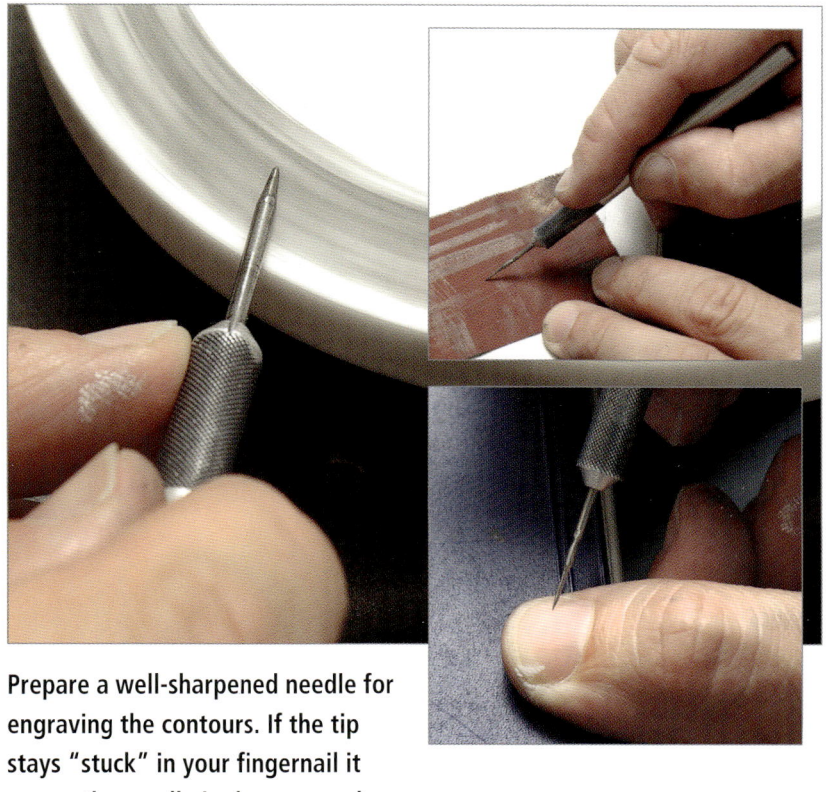

Prepare a well-sharpened needle for engraving the contours. If the tip stays "stuck" in your fingernail it means the needle is sharp enough.

I usually start on one side and then work my way step by step to the opposite side. Keep your design close to the piece. This serves as an "interim control" and enhances your sense of the work.

Another little tip: Avoid having too sharp of a breaking edge on the needle tip. The needle slides more easily around curves and subtle roundings when it has been cleanly polished round.

Now comes an exciting moment: Removing the opaque white primer shows whether you have worked cleanly and diligently so far. Before coloring you have to wipe the piece thoroughly. First, use a soft, slightly damp cloth. You can finish cleaning using a

Use especial care when pre-engraving the contours. Make sure you do not forget any line.

little nail polish remover. However, test the remover first on a hidden part of the piece, making sure the material will not be discolored or the surface is otherwise affected.

It can be rather difficult if you have forgotten any of the contours. In this case, you should already stain the existing contours. The area where the lines are missing should be partially re-coated with some opaque white using a cotton swab. Then place the tracing paper template accurately over the work once again, fasten the paper securely, and rub over the appropriate places again.

HOW TO USE THE ENGRAVING NEEDLE

It is best to hold an engraving needle as you would a pencil or pen. It is important to clasp the front part of the needle—the part right below the tip—firmly with the thumb and index finger. These two fingers should hold and guide the needle. The ring finger serves as the "finger pad" for the needle.

Never hold an engraving needle cramped too tightly. Try to guide the needle in a relaxed way. When scribing deeper structures, the pressure you need to remove material from the piece's surface should come mainly from the thumb tip. Always use smooth movements.

A little exercise to start: Take the needle in your hand as if you wanted to start an engraving. Now put the heels of your hands lightly on the surface of the table and raise the needle tip, so it is in the air. Make loose, circular motions in the air with the needle. Write some imaginary sentences in the air. This relaxes the hand. If you notice that you cannot hold the needle comfortably at a specific place, or that it cuts or leaves bruises, wrap the needle with some tape (masking tape) at that place. Wrapping it is also helpful when a needle is too thin; the tape helps you grasp and guide it better.

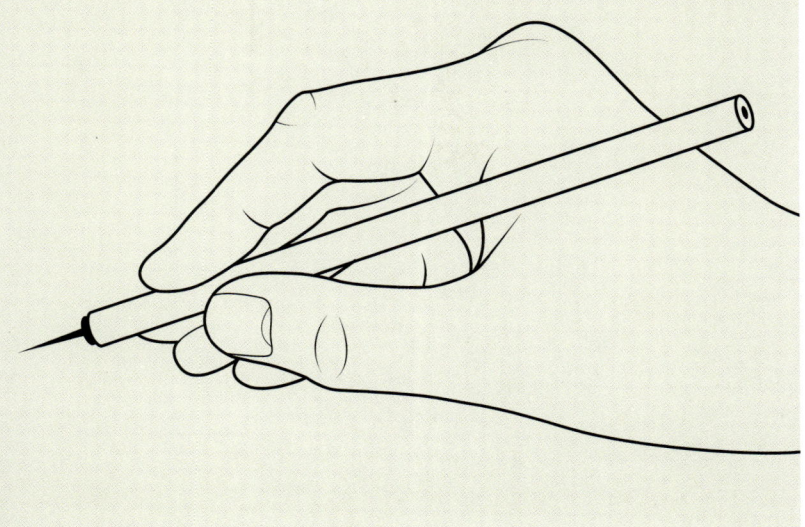

Under magnification it is easy to see that an engraved line raises fine shavings. This is a good way to check whether the corresponding place has already been scribed.

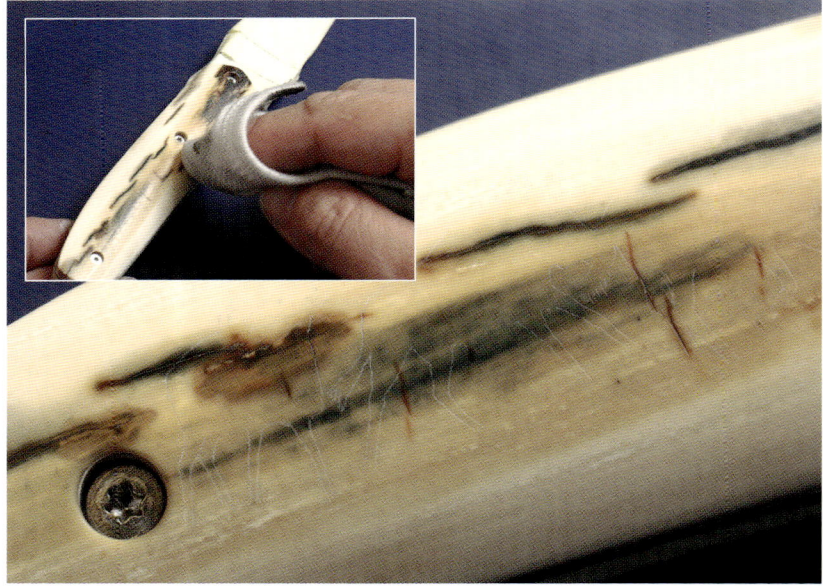

After initially scribing the contours, the opaque white is removed with a damp cloth. Repeat the process if necessary to remove any pigment residue. The polished surface of the material must again reflect light.

4.7 Applying the Pigment

It is possible to color the engraving in several different ways. A very common method is using cotton swabs. The cotton swab is saturated with the desired pigment, then you can very carefully and selectively apply the color with light pressure where it is needed. This allows you to work and color in sections.

Then you can rub the pigment with a soft cotton cloth. Find a clean spot on your cloth and wipe the excess pigment from the engraved surface.

When, where, and how often you apply pigment depends on the subject, the material, and the skill of the individual. I almost always start with the darker areas of a scene; this way, I quickly get a feeling for the material. Then I color these areas right away, to see how they hold the pigment.

There can be several reasons why something does not work well. Below, I list the two most common problems and their causes.

The pigment does not adhere: Maybe the needle used to engrave the lines was too blunt. The nature of the pigment may also play a role. It could be the pigment was diluted too much. Another possibility is that the type of pigment applied did not harmonize with the material being engraved and adheres badly. Therefore, it is important to always test the pigment you are using beforehand. If the pigment does not adhere well, I advise using a more viscous, paste-like consistency. It may be due to the material's surface; always make sure it is free of grease.

The color of the engraving after coloring is a different grey or other tone than desired: To fix this, you must change the density or depth of the engraved structures. This is not easy for a beginner. Each material behaves differently and each subject is different. You have to keep readjusting your work over and over, depending on the circumstances. Experience is enormously important here.

Apply the pigment with a cotton swab. All engraved lines have to be completely covered with the pigment.

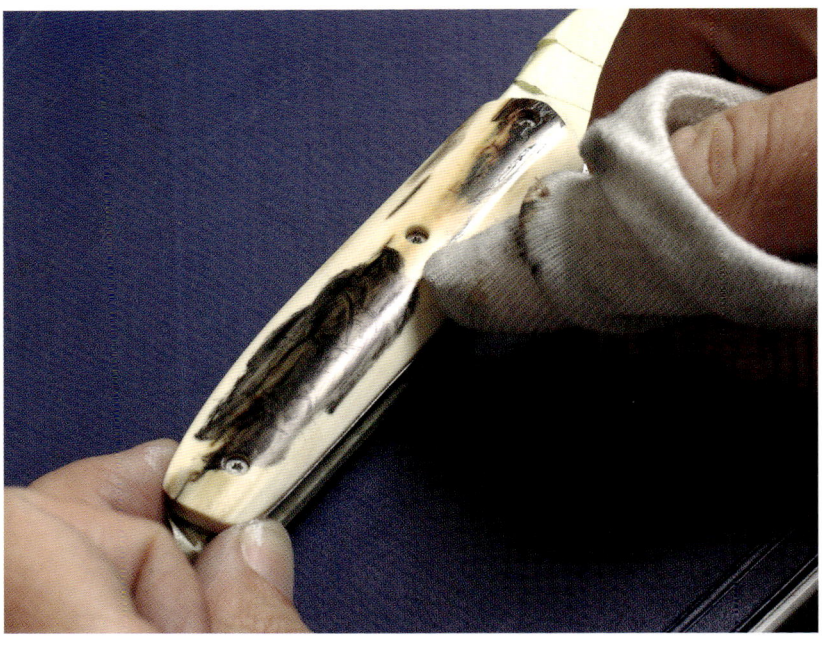

Next, wipe off the excess pigment immediately with a soft cotton cloth.

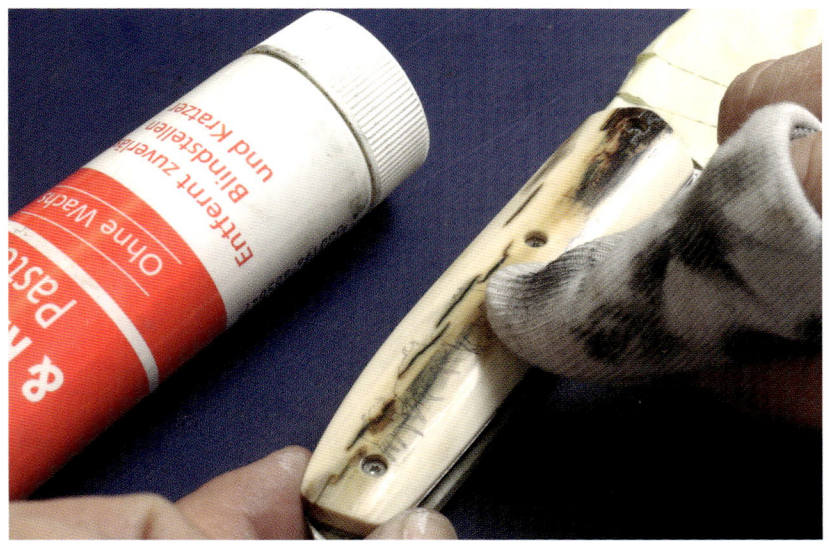

In the next step, the entire work surface is re-polished until it reflects light.

The colored guide lines can now be easily seen on the gleaming surface of the material.

85

4.8 Mapping Out the Border Lines

When I am working out the subject design, I first lay out the contours and relevant internal border points and lines. In this way, I create for myself a "rough" framework for the subject in its various levels and areas.

Clearly defined border lines are vital for a clean result. Again, I begin on the darker parts and slowly work my way through the various shades of gray to light gray. For a grizzly bear portrait, I would first start work on the outer contours, then basically define the eyes, and then later the nose, the contour lines in the ear area, and so on.

If you have done clean initial work on these sections it is much easier to "fill in" the larger sections. Whether you use dots or shade them in with cross-hatching depends on the result you want to achieve. More on that in the next section.

I like to re-engrave the border lines with a rather blunt-angled needle to deepen them.

Once again, the re-engraved part of the engraving is partially re-colored using a cotton swab. At this point, the polished background on the material's surface will not absorb any more pigment.

After coloring and wiping off the excess, you can see clearly that the deeper re-engraved lines appear darker.

HOW TO USE A GRAVER

The graver used for hand engraving consists of the actual steel blade and the grip piece, the so-called graver handle. To work with the hand graver, it is important to know how to hold and guide it. Hold the knob (the handle or grip end) of the graver in your right fist (for left-handers, the following description refers to the left hand). The thumb is extended and held sideways against the graver. Position the index finger across from the thumb. This creates a holding position that stabilizes the graver. The fingers can also influence the angle that you hold the graver.

Grip the graver handle securely with your remaining fingers at the ball of your thumb. Place the graver onto a sample piece of your material. The tip should be applied gently and carefully. Now comes the difficult part: push the graver carefully forward, millimeter by millimeter. Use only gentle pressure. It is advisable to start by engraving simple straight lines on a test piece. By tilting the graver and a corresponding wrist movement, you can engrave curves. Try not to press too hard with the hand graver, otherwise you will bore deep too quickly.

My advice is to first try some sample engravings. This can take quite some time. Do not lose patience, and always remember that you should keep a loose and relaxed grip on the hand graver.

A little tip: At first, use the hand graver more for short lines and dots. It is technically easier to make these structures. This way, over time you will get used to using this tool and can do better and easier work with practice.

Then you can star working on more complicated engraved designs.

Now we begin to fill the surface areas with closely set dots. A needle polished to a sharp angle is helpful here.

Keep checking by repeatedly re-coloring. The engraver uses feel and experience to decide how often to do this.

After wiping off the pigment, the colored dots are visible as a dense black area.

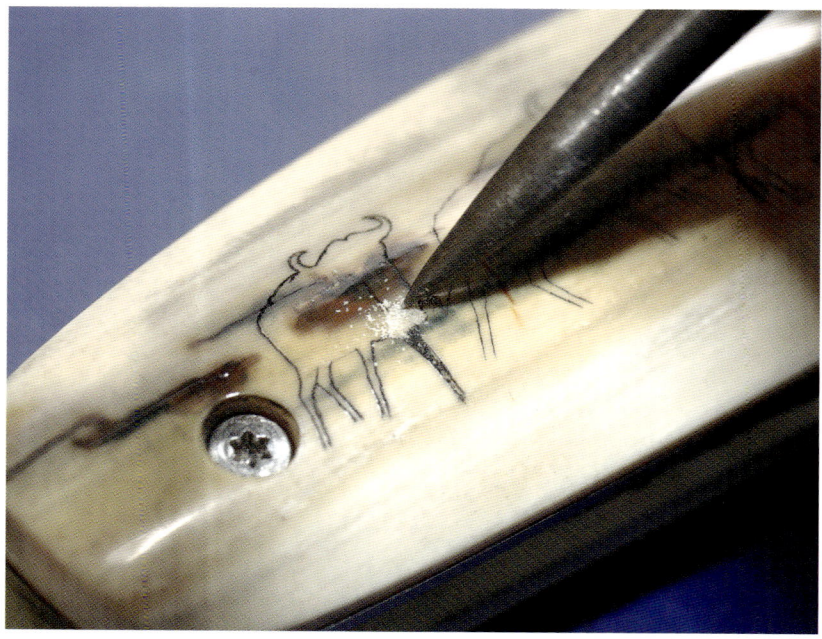

You can also use a needle with a blunter angle to fill in spaces with dots.

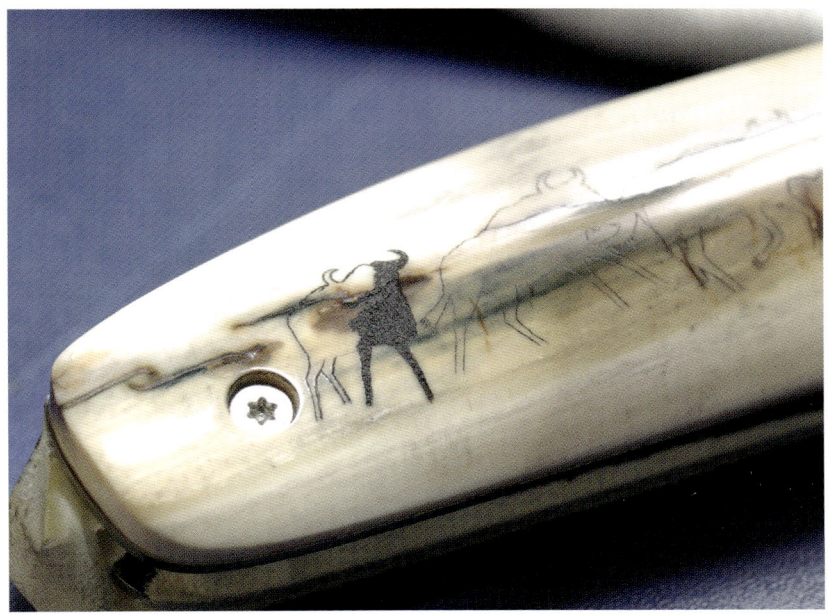

It is best to work dot by dot, from one side forward to the other side. As a right-hander, I work from right to left.

When the area is colored, the uniformly deep and close-set dots yield a uniform black.

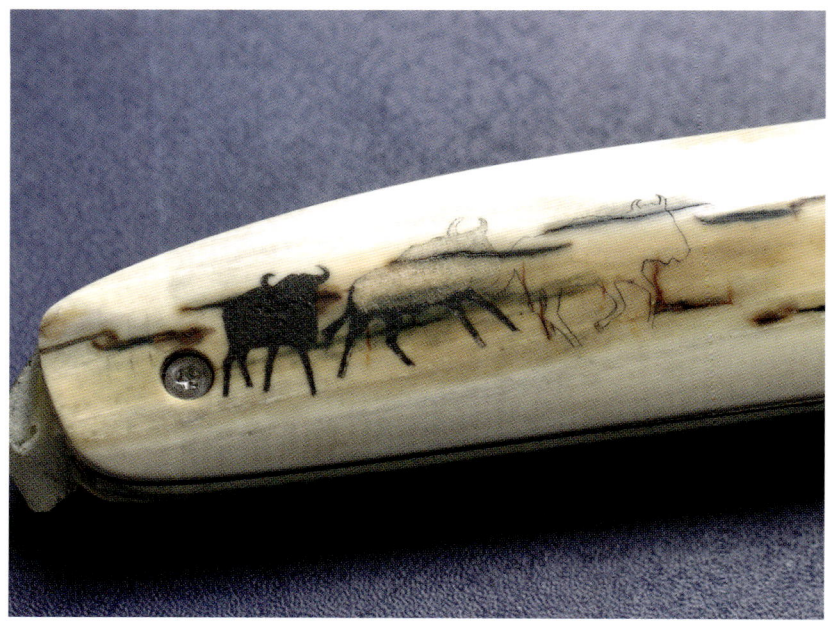

Dot by dot, we engrave the next gnu in our African design; here, I work from bottom (the legs) to top.

The individual surfaces are stippled slowly but steadily. The design is created.

Keep on checking the stippled dots in the light from your lamp before coloring.

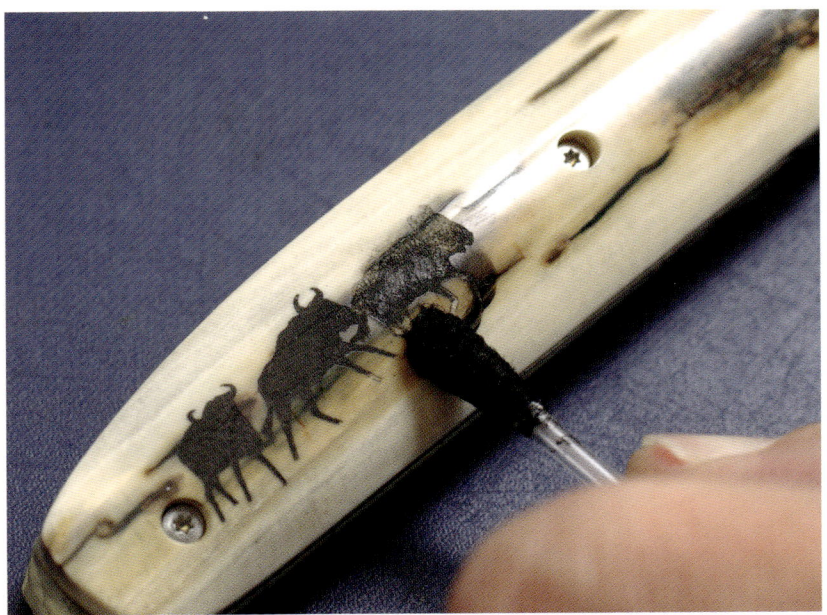

Finally, blacken the gnu again using cotton swabs and pigment.

To make additional changes in the design at the bottom of the handle we gently pat on opaque white using our fingers.

Now you can draw with a pencil. With simple guide lines you can do this without having to do further free-hand.

We draw in some grass turf as an underlay for the gnu herd as a series of short, irregular vertical lines.

Now we carefully engrave the penciled lines. Again, take care not to forget any lines!

Carefully wipe away the opaque white with the cloth.

Again, the guide lines are blackened in with cotton swab and pigment.

The blades of grass indicated by the guide lines are now clearly visible.

Now we begin to engrave blade for blade out of the surface of the material.

The density and depth of the lines also determine the gray tone obtained after coloring.

Here you can see the difference between the black color scheme (gnus) and the gray of the blades of grass.

4.9 Surface Area Techniques

4.9.1 Stippling Technique

Using the stippling technique involves gridding the surface area with needle or graver, creating a structure of fine dots. This lets you obtain very fine results and achieve excellent light-dark transitions. The density and depth of the dots determines the degree of shading.

The stippling technique lets you represent almost any type of surface. This technique is very time consuming, as you only progress "point by point" in the truest sense of the words.

You can create different effects, depending on the cut of the needle or graver. For darker, deeper structures, I like to use a somewhat stronger needle with a slightly faceted tip. This makes

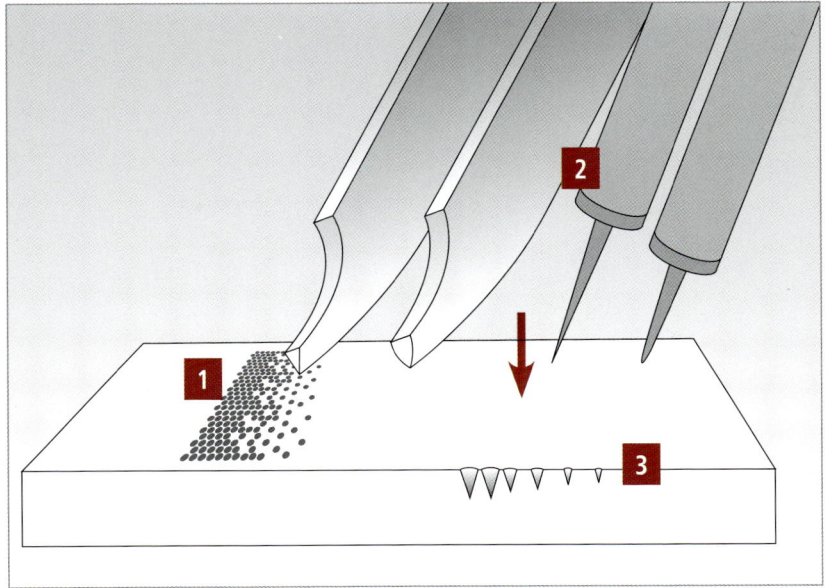

Stippling technique: Depending on the density (1) and depth (3) of the dots engraved with a needle or graver (2), coloring yields different gray or black effects.

it possible to make a pyramid-shaped impression—as viewed under magnification. These will hold the pigment very well. If you "overlap" the dots, you will get an even better rich black color effect. I use a needle with a blunter angle to engrave densely set dots intended to create a lighter gray effect.

A tip: Test your tool and the desired effect on a piece of sample material—ideally the same material as your piece.

For the stippling technique, the needle is pushed in light up-and-down movements into the surface. Hold the needle loosely between the forefinger and thumb, as you would a pencil. The emphasis is on loosely! If you grip too tightly, you will tense up quickly. You will eventually determine how quickly you do your stippling work. For larger, uniformly black areas you can make a sport of it, to see how quickly you progress. I like to interrupt work on larger, uniformly black areas, because this can very easily become monotonous.

It becomes more difficult when stippling transition areas. Here, the depth and density of the dots determines the tone of the gray you create. I also begin here mostly with black, to get a feel for the dots and the material. Then I work my way slowly to the lighter tones.

4.9.2 Line Technique

Line technique is the most widely used and most traditional technique for scrimshaw engraving. Surfaces are filled with lines of different density and depth. It is up to the engraver to determine the level of detail they want to engrave.

You should decide whether to use lines or dots, depending on the subject and the desired effect. It makes little sense to engrave fur or hair structures with dots; here, lines have much more to offer. Engraving deeper lines often requires using some more force;

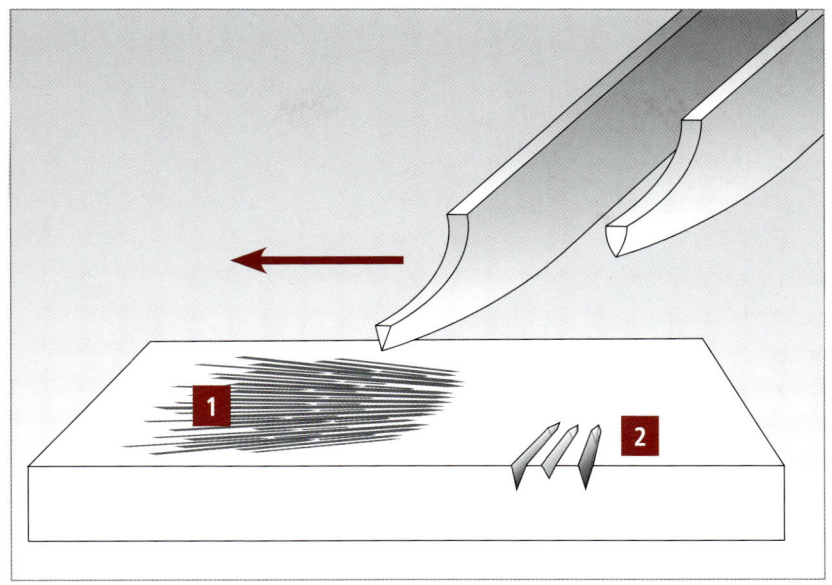

Line technique: Lines, depending on the desired effect, can be drawn in different directions and depths (1). Here again, the formula holds that density and depth (2) determine light-dark values later on.

finer lines, however, demand a corresponding skill and a really sure and steady hand from the engraver.

I've learned that needles with cut facets are good tools to cut deeper lines into material. The more acute the angle of the needle point—whether faceted or not—the better it is for engraving fine lines. The blunter the angle, the more suitable the needle is for deeper lines. However, the angle should not be more than 45 degrees.

Lines can be engraved slightly apart in cross-hatching, or they may overlap. They can be made shorter or longer. It is up to the artist to decide.

I recommend that any budding scrimshaw engraver prepare a test piece. To begin, carve a diamond pattern about 0.4" apart with a

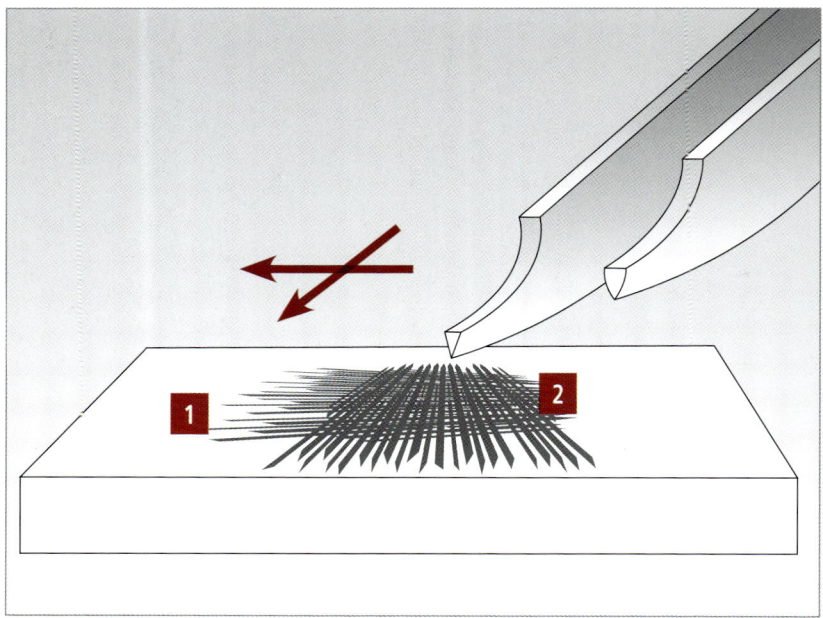

Cross-hatching technique: By cross-hatching lines (1) you obtain greater density in the engraving. By using different angles as you overlay the lines and the depth of engraving, you will achieve light-dark gradations (2) after coloring.

steel ruler. You can then fill in each of these diamonds with lines. Try to give each area a different shade of gray by making the lines in each area a different depth or density. Anyone who has completed this exercise is ready for their first free-form design. If you haven't succeeded in this exercise yet, you should repeat it until you have.

4.9.3 Cross-hatch Technique

The cross-hatch technique is an elaboration of line technique. As the name suggests, the lines cross one upon the other in different layers or angles. As in line technique, the depth and density determine the resulting light-dark effect. I use the cross-hatch technique when I want to fill in very dark areas, such as if I want to surround an animal subject in the foreground with areas of black.

HOW TO USE A PUNCH AND HAMMER

Using an engraving punch is comparable to carefully hammering a nail held on a horizontal surface. Hold the punch in your left hand (if you are right-handed). With your forefinger and middle finger on one side and your thumb on the other side of the punch you can keep it well under control. Ideally, hold the punch with the tip perpendicular to the surface of the piece. You can also hold the punch at an angle as required.

The right hand holds the engraving hammer. This way, your right-hand fist is around the handle end of the hammer. The index finger should be held above to better guide the hammer handle, with the thumb held as a counter-weight below or beside the thumb.

Now try to hammer the punch with springy, light strokes. The "art" is to move the punch a little further after each stroke. Slight impressions from the tip of the punch should appear next to each other on the material's surface. The density and depth, and the form of the punch tip, determine the ultimate light-dark effect that emerges after coloring. Punching requires some practice in advance, but it can be an efficient technique, such as for filling in a background quickly.

I recommend you collect some commercially available steel punches for your tool kit. You can always re-grind the punch tips as needed. I frequently change the angle of the tip to match the requirements of each scrimshaw engraving.

The cross lines do not have to run 100% parallel. This allows for relatively informal work. It also moves ahead quite quickly. For this technique, I highly recommend you try your first cross-hatched lines on a sample piece before moving on to other designs.

4.9.4 Punch Technique

One exciting method is using an engraving punch and hammer to stipple dots and structures. Both hands are required for this technique, and coordinating your hands is the challenge. The hammer is held in the right hand, the punch in the left.

Conceptualize the situation as if you wanted to hammer a nail into a board—the only difference is that you keep moving the nail from one place to the next and that you must strike very carefully.

You structure the material's surface by striking on the constantly moving punch. You obtain the corresponding light and dark effect depending on how firmly you make the stroke and the density of the structures created in the material. I think the punching technique is more suitable for the advanced engraver. Anyone who masters it, however, can create beautiful effects.

4.9.5 Mezzotint

In mezzotint technique, only fine layers of the material are scraped off the surface. You usually obtain a more or less light shade of gray after coloring. This method can be used effectively if you do not want any white in a background. I like to scrape the background first gently, then color the area in and then cross-hatch, stipple, or use a punch over it. This creates a strong depth effect.

The best-suited tools are scalpels or other fine knives. It is important that your tool has sharp edges. Improvisation is called for here.

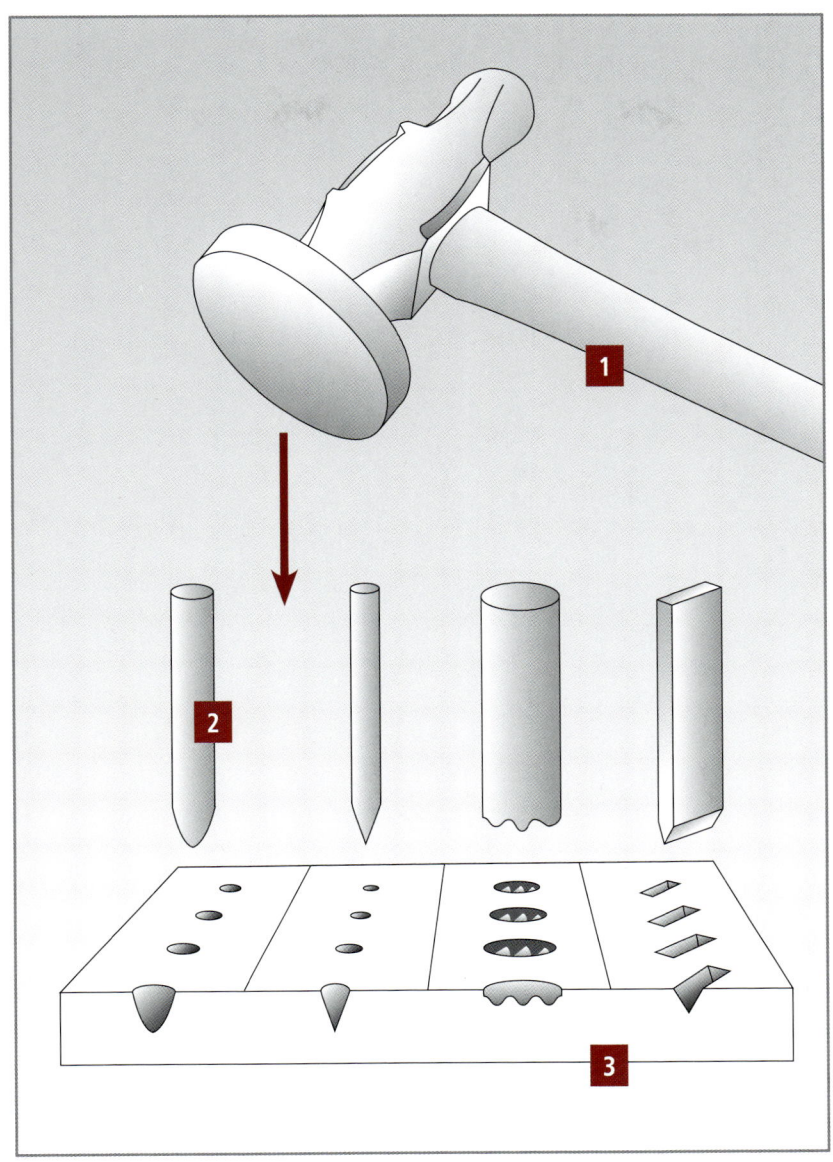

Punch technique: You create an impression in the material (3) by striking with the hammer (1) on a punch (2). It is important to keep the punch as upright as possible.

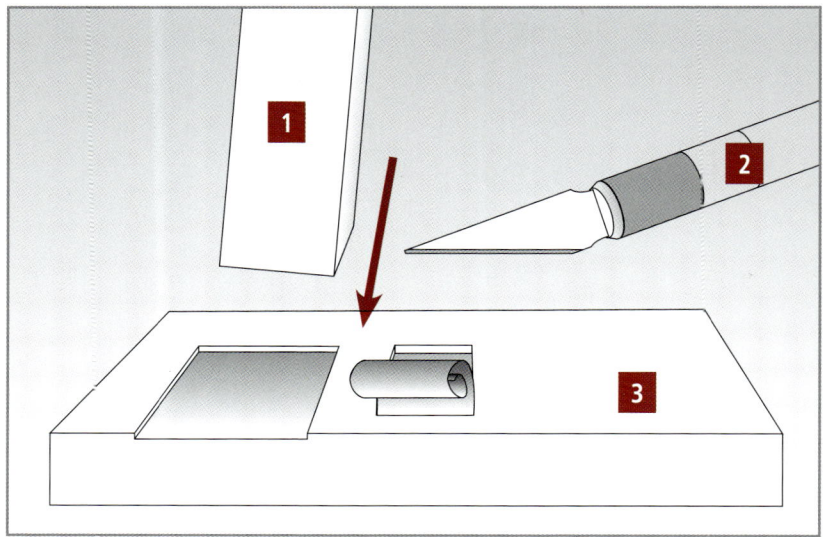

Mezzotint technique: With sharpened square steel (1) or scalpel blades (2) you can scrape off the top layers of many materials (3). Make sure you are putting uniform pressure on the tool and scrape the surface lightly.

Try out several knives or square steels, which have edges that are wonderfully suited for such purposes. A flat-edged graver also works very well, but it requires more practice.

4.9.6 Combining Techniques

I find that mixing the techniques listed is the most exciting way to work. Combining is the way to achieve the most interesting effects. If you were previously only playing one "instrument," now you are conducting a "small orchestra." The possibilities are almost limitless.

But that presupposes you have mastered each technique. I therefore recommend that every scrimshaw engraver first devote themselves to learning each basic technique before moving on to combining techniques.

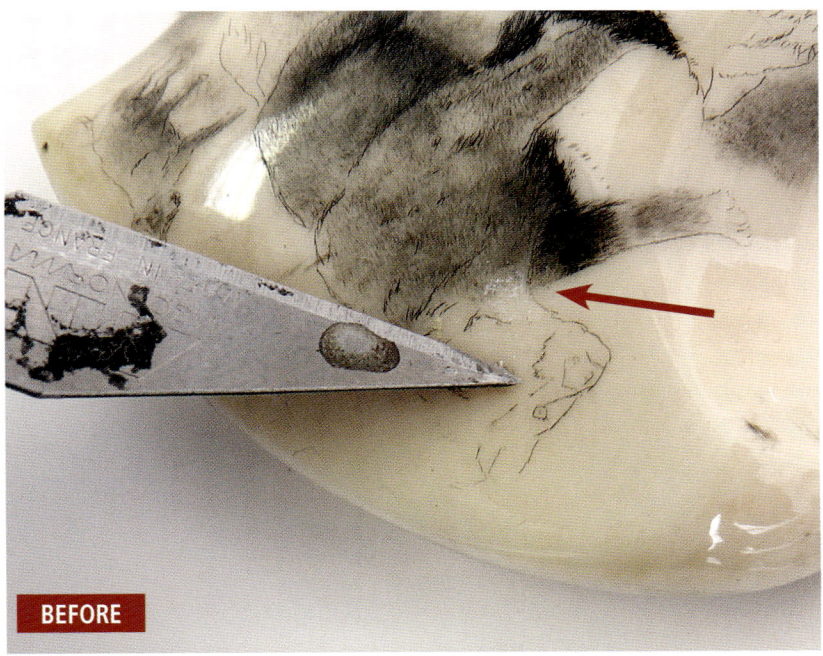

BEFORE

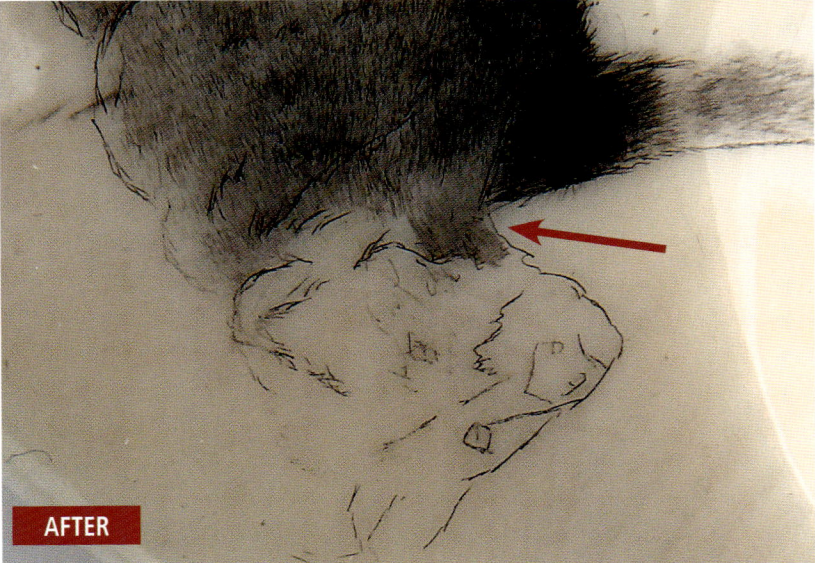

AFTER

After coloring, you can achieve uniformly dense and bright tones using the mezzotint technique. Tip: First rub the scalpel over coarse sandpaper. This will give you a micro-fine "saw-tooth" effect when scraping the surface of the material.

4.10 Brightening up the Engraving

A very special art of scrimshaw engraving is brightening up the work you have done. This can be accomplished in many different ways, depending mainly on what work is to be lightened and with what goal.

If an engraved surface is to be brightened because it simply has become too dark after coloring, you can rub the whole surface gently with a cotton cloth and acrylic polish. The intensity of the polishing determines the degree of lightening. Use a careful and slow touch. Here, experience and a sure instinct are required.

If the surfaces are smaller, or even set in the middle of the design, you can apply polish using a cotton swab and carefully attempt the process this way. In really tiny areas, you get the best effect by applying polish to a very sharp toothpick and polish as if you were working with a pencil lead.

The second possibility is that you deliberately want to brighten up the work you have done. This may be necessary if you want to create highlights. A burnishing needle can be a good aid for this purpose. With this tool, you can scrape out specific areas in the engraving. Depending on the intensity, this brings the basic material to light. This effect can be used very well if you want to cover dark fur or hair structures with lighter hair. It is important, though, that you always do this at the end of the scrimshaw engraving process. Under no circumstances should you re-color afterwards, because this will simply eliminate this effect.

4.11 Creating Transitions

Creating transitions is the most advanced school of scrimshaw. The aim is to produce a harmonious graduation from light to dark in the engraved scrimshaw design. There are several ways you

BEFORE

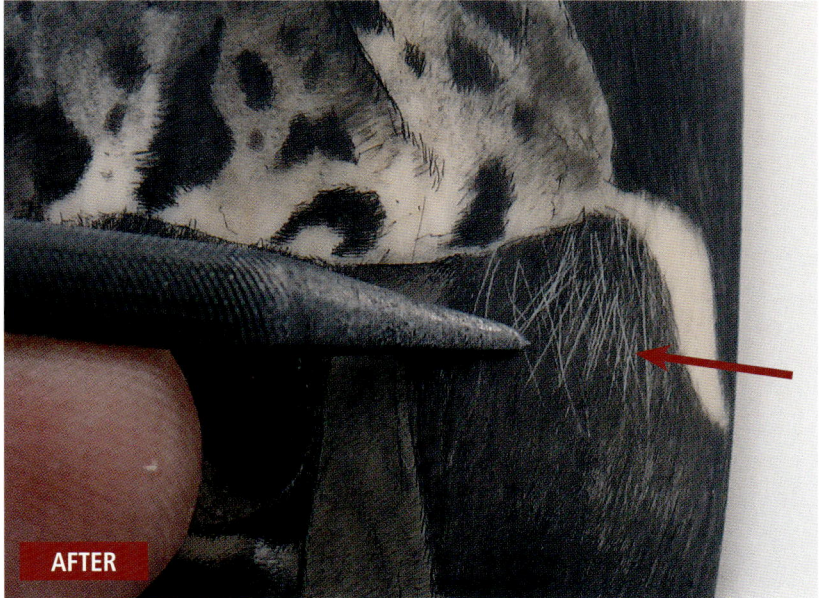

AFTER

A needle honed to a slightly obtuse angle is ideal for scratching out light lines from a densely engraved, dark-colored area of work. This effect can be used very well for engraving grass or fur.

can pursue this goal. The first way is to change the structure in the depth of the engraving work. The deeper you engrave a dot, the darker it will be after coloring. Depending on the type of material and its texture, you have to test every single piece for the effect created by the depth of the engraving after coloring.

Another possibility is to structure the engraved work by density. The further apart dots or lines are set, the brighter the work you have created will appear.

A third method is to combine these two methods. More wide-set, lightly engraved lines and dots yield lighter structures, while deeper and closer-set lines and dots yield a darker effect.

The proof of the pudding is in the eating. Prepare a "training piece" of your favorite materials and get started.

The combination of different techniques—if you have really mastered each individual technique—leads to a real work of art with an amazingly natural effect.

ON COLLECTING SCRIMSHAW

Scrimshaw is a passion. Once you have caught the "virus," scrimshaw can be an addiction (not dangerous to your health). The interesting thing is not owning one or more objects, but your involvement with them. If an engraved object is set in its intended place, it is always gleaming at its owner. Often collectors tell me their engravings give them renewed joy all the time. So much for the philosophical part.

Anyone who has decided to collect scrimshaw art should also take note of other issues. One of the most important is: Where do I put my collection? Keep in mind that the objects should never be kept in any place that is too dry. Humidity should be at least forty-five percent. Direct sunlight should also be avoided. The engraved materials may crack if kept in the wrong place, and grip panels can contract. One inappropriate place is directly over an open fireplace that is used regularly.

I have heard of collectors who only store their object in a vault. I think it is a shame to keep such objects hidden from the eye. Other collectors keep telling me of the pleasure it gives them each day to be able to look at their small scrimshaw collection when entering their office, which always makes the day begin well. I am always happy when I hear something like that, because that certainly represents the deeper meaning of this art.

Sometimes I am asked how best to begin collecting scrimshaw. Well, quite simply: Look out for appropriate objects and start by purchasing your first one. But this is easy to say. I think your approach to the subject of scrimshaw is important. I know a collector who actually had no interest at all in scrimshaw as an art form. His passion was collecting elephants.

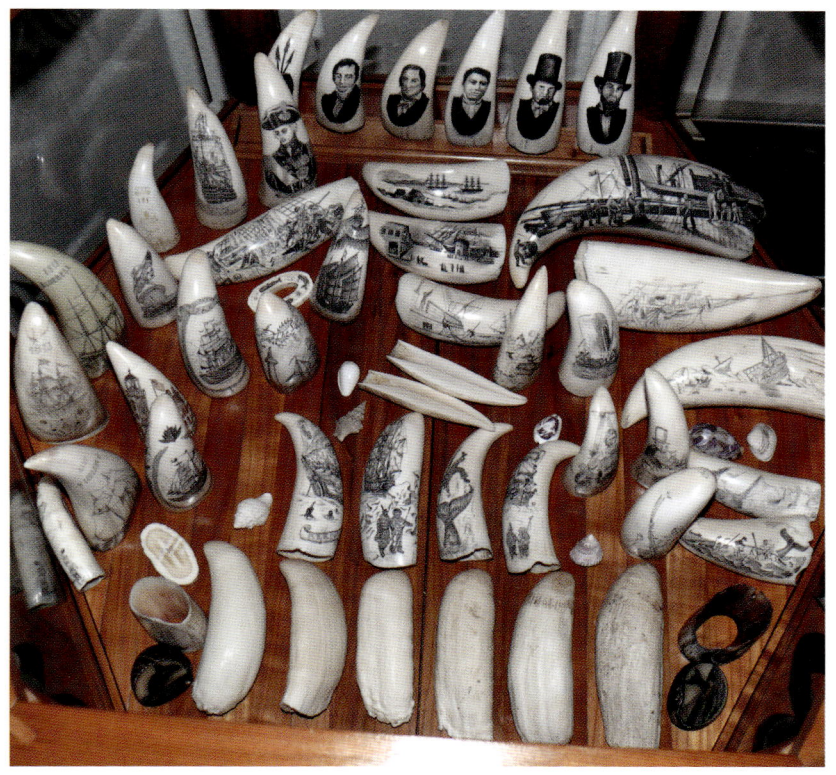

Antique pieces have often been collected and gathered together over decades. The collector often changes over the years, whether he focuses purely on maritime or on specialized themes.

After he had seen an elephant engraved in scrimshaw for the first time, he had to have it in his collection. Then others followed.

Other collectors focus on maritime art. Scrimshaw with maritime designs then almost automatically become an integral part of such a collection. Still other people stumble by chance on an exhibition or a book about this art form and are fascinated by the subtlety of these miniature works of art.

From whichever direction you approach the theme, I think it is worth it when you become engaged in dealing with scrimshaw beforehand. Read books on the subject and consult the Internet. Often a personal conversation with an artist or dealer is an important step. The best results come about if the customer and artist can intensively exchange ideas beforehand on the subject of an engraving.

Fortunately, their tastes are different. What one person likes for a long time another may not accept. I well remember an incident when I started working as an engraver: I exhibited some of my first scrimshaw work at a hunting fair. A prospective customer, who introduced himself as a hunter and nature expert, examined an engraved red deer. He found it actually quite successful, but then declared that the antlers did not quite fit the size of the body. He said goodbye and walked on. The next day, another interested buyer came to the booth. As it turned out, also a sportsman. He saw this deer and waxed lyrical: The most beautiful deer he had ever seen....

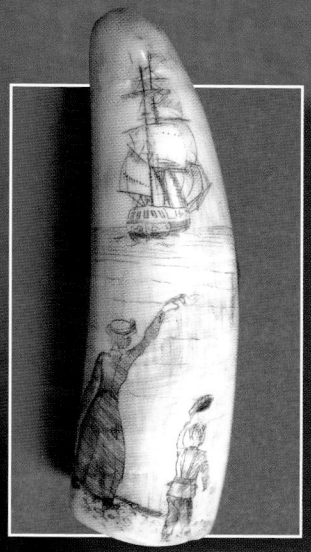

Scrimshaw in its original form, naive and impressive. These maritime works of art from earlier periods can often only be admired in museum collections

CONCLUDING REMARKS

I am sure that some readers have already begun taking the first steps to making an engraving while reading. This book is certainly intended as a "practical experience book." A book that you always keep getting out to look up something and then leaf through it. I have tried to introduce the reader slowly and in simple steps to the subject of scrimshaw.

Of course, when you are actually doing the practical work, new detailed questions will keep coming up. It is the same for me: I hardly have a day when I don't find myself facing a new technical or artistic challenge. Sometimes I spend the entire night wondering how to solve a technical problem. On other days, it takes only minutes to find a solution.

Each material is different, as is each design and its creation. There is an infinite number of different pathways to follow. How is it said so beautifully? The journey is its own reward. In terms of scrimshaw engraving, I can only confirm this.

Do not despair if something does not work out the way you would like. Never try to reach your goal by using force. If a piece just starts to go badly, then put it aside and work on another. Treat yourself to just a few days' time away from it. Do not worry; within that time, you will not have forgotten or unlearned everything. No, you will realize that things go better afterwards and you will take up the work with new elan and fresh ideas on the matter. Scrimshaw takes time: time for the artist to develop it and time to create an engraving.

Scrimshaw will always take you to your limits. The longer you are intensively occupied with it, the more you will develop with the challenges. Take pleasure in those you meet and it will always work out for you.

I wish you much pleasure with the art of scrimshaw engraving and invite you to enjoy the following gallery of a selection of engraving work. Perhaps it might inspire you.

I want to thank here all the friends and enthusiasts of this art form who bore me company from the beginning and constantly encouraged me. Not to forget Egon Trompeter, who has been a longtime friend and business partner, and shared his own knowledge with me.

December 2009

Richard "Ritchi" Maier

GALLERY

I have compiled some of my scrimshaw work on the following pages. These include different designs and engraving techniques. I hope that in this way, I can give you an overview of the spectrum of my work and this will encourage your own ideas.

"Bear Family"
(Fossil mammoth ivory, piece of tooth)
Because of the intensive basic color of the material, only one design in "backlight" was possible, as far as I was concerned, with soft contrasts and limited light reflections. Bears are a good option on a highly colored surface. The "light source" in the background was the only bright spot in this mammoth ivory tooth fragment.

"Tiger Face"
(Fossil mammoth ivory, stabilized, on ebony base)
I always carve at least two "layers" for animals that have spots or stripes.
The first layer is the tiger without its stripes. In the second layer, I overlay
the stripes and spots in the fur. The whiskers are left light and hollow.
This also means that all dark areas around the whiskers—just a few tenths
wide—are engraved. This is a time-consuming and technically challenging
operation.

"Chamois"
(Fossil mammoth ivory, stabilized)
The eye plays a central role in this design, with its various shadings. Due to the white background of mammoth ivory, I created the light passages in the chamois' fur by using different light shades of gray, to produce a contrast.

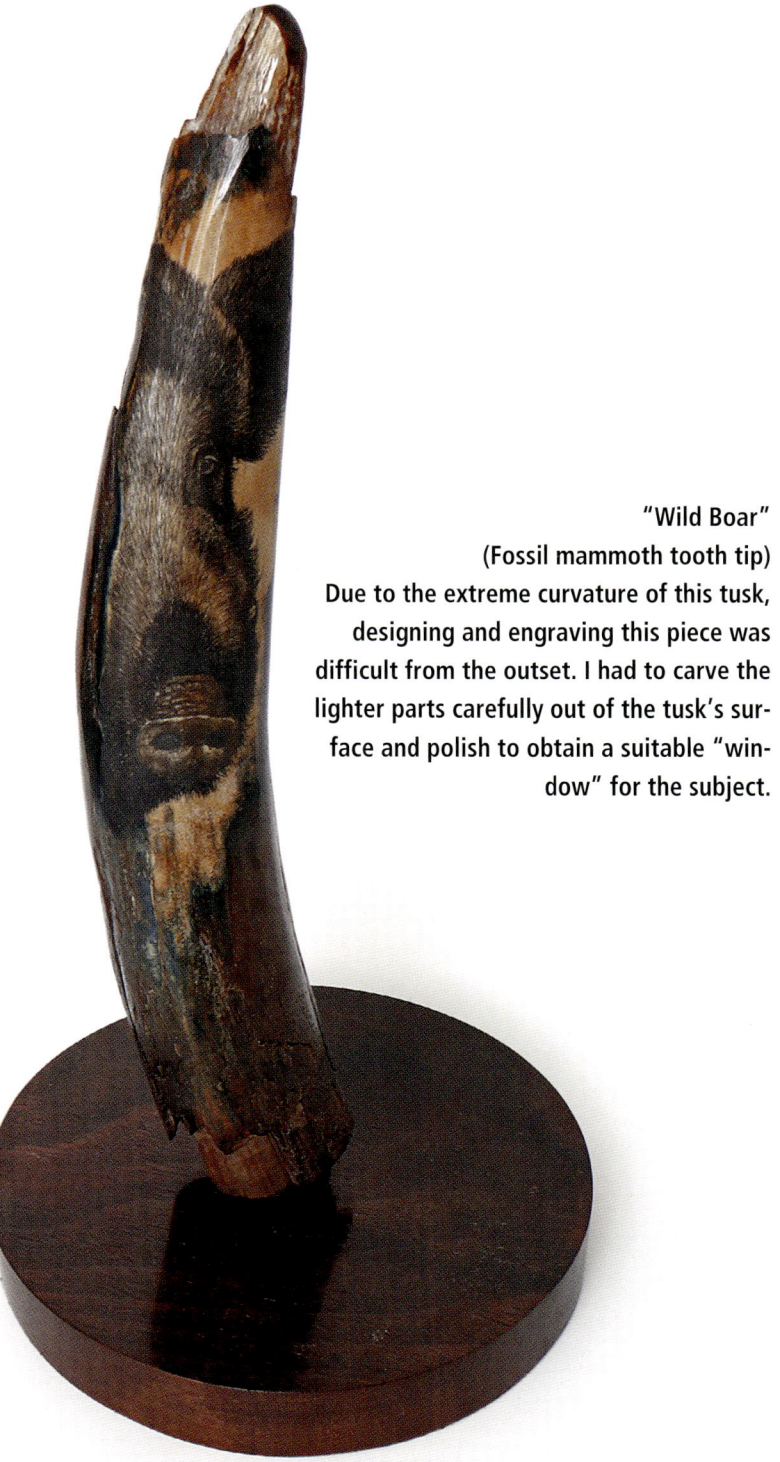

"Wild Boar"
(Fossil mammoth tooth tip)
Due to the extreme curvature of this tusk, designing and engraving this piece was difficult from the outset. I had to carve the lighter parts carefully out of the tusk's surface and polish to obtain a suitable "window" for the subject.

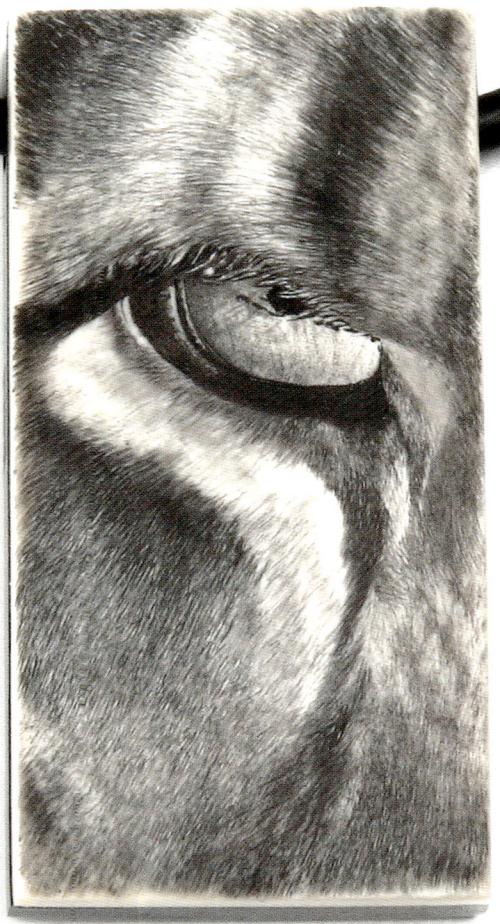

"Lion Eye"
(Pendant, fossil mammoth ivory, stabilized)
Animal eyes fascinate me. I like to carve them on
pendants and try to capture the "soul" behind
the eye and reproduce it.

"Cougar"
(Fossil mammoth ivory, stabilized)
The face and fur structure of a cougar are marked by different color tones
and hair lengths. The "art" is to also capture the majesty of his being in
the engraving.

"Elephant and Lion" from the collection "Big 5"
(Fossil mammoth ivory on ebony base)
This mammoth tusk, some 18½ inches high (without base), was a particular challenge. First, it was necessary to fill in some 153 square inches of flat area. If you calculate the progress of a scrimshaw engraving in millimeters, this was a very time-consuming task. Another difficulty was to integrate the curvature into the draft design. I also had to take surface staining and cracks in the material into consideration.

"Hunting Dog"
(Hunting knife by Toni Gruber, fossil mammoth
ivory, stabilized) Hunters are happy to have their
hunting dogs carved on the handles of their
knives. Work like this requires a microscope
or a good magnifying glass.

"Zebrasimba"
(Bracelet, fossil mammoth ivory)
The design of the bracelet consisted of the high-contrast pattern of zebra skins and hunting lions. The gray tones of the lions form a counterpoint to the black and white of the zebras.

"Lion Head"
(Fossil mammoth ivory, stabilized, on ebony base)
This lion engraving interested me particularly through the play of light and shadow in its presentation. It is rare to show male lions in a profile view. By keeping the background dark, the contours of the head are highlighted particularly well against the play of light and shadow. However, it was very time consuming to do the stippling for the background.

"Leopard Head"
(Fossil mammoth ivory on
ebony base, from the
"Big 5" collection)
The dimensions of this
leopard head almost
correspond to those of a
real animal. This work is the
centerpiece of the "Big 5
collection." I attempted to
present the eye so that it
fixes on the viewer. As I was
working, carving out the
head became entwined with
the surface structure
of the tusk.

"Hunting Dog" and "Falcon"
(Pendants, fossil mammoth ivory)
Often customers have their own
idea for a scrimshaw engraving
which can then be engraved on a
pendant, for example.

"Ibex"
(Fossil mammoth ivory, stabilized, on wooden base)
Incorporating motifs into the structures and colors of the surface material is an exciting challenge every time. The snow-capped mountain in the middle of the background was the lightest part of the mammoth tooth. I laid out the design in such a way that I could use this area as a "snowfield."

"The Wolf in My Mind"
(Fossil mammoth ivory on ebony base)
The wolf's essence is unfathomable.
have a special connection to this animal. In this engraving I have tried
to present the light-dark interplay
so that the wolf's muzzle
stands out from
the material.

"Impala"
(Fossil mammoth ivory, stabilized)
In this engraving I was inspired by the legend of St. Hubertus.
The Hubertus stag appears in the legend with an illuminated
crucifix between its antlers. In my impala, the "eye of the
hunter" looks through the antlers as a lion's eye.

"Falcon"
(Fossil mammoth ivory on
ebony base)
The weathered tip of a
mammoth tooth gave me the
idea for a hawk. I used the
lighter areas in the middle
of the tooth for the natural
coloring of the falcon's feathers.
I used the brownish color
patches behind the falcon to
represent dark clouds in the
background.

"Racing Yacht"
(Fossil mammoth ivory, stabilized, on ebony base)
Engravings of sailing ships with rigging and moving waves are a special technical challenge. Already in the design and sketching very precise work was required for this engraving. Working out the fine script in the context of the curvature requires good spatial imagination.

"Cape Buffalo" (Fossil mammoth ivory on ebony base)
African animals—especially the "Big 5"—are a recurring theme in my scrimshaw. The "Big 5" are the elephant, buffalo, rhino, lion, and leopard.

"Rhino"
(Fossil mammoth ivory on ebony base)
To represent an animal from a "worm's eye view" always creates additional
tension in a scene. Right by a rhinoceros, the viewer gets the impression
that they are lying right in front of the animal in the grass.

APPENDIX

8.1 Books about Scrimshaw

- *Modernes Scrimshaw* (Eva Halat)

- *Scrimshaw Techniques* (Jim Stevens)

- *Advanced Scrimshaw Techniques* (Jim Stevens)

- *Scrimshaw: A Complete Illustrated Manual* (Steve Paszkiewicz and Roger Schroeder)

- *Learning How to Scrimshaw* (Ron Newton)

- *A Treasury of American Scrimshaw: A Collection of the Useful and Decorative* (Michael McManus)

- *How to Scrimshaw and Carve Ivory* (Blackie Collins and Michael Collins)

- *Scrimshaw: The Whaler's Legacy* (Martha Lawrence)

- *Scrimshaw* - Little craft book series (Carson IA Ritchie)

- *Nautical Illustrations: 681 Permission-Free Illustrations from Nineteenth-Century Sources* – Dover Pictorial Archive Series (Jim Harter)

- *Ready-to-Use Old-Fashioned Nautical Illustrations* – Dover Clip-Art Series (Carol Belanger Grafton)

- *The Second Scrimshaw Connection* (Bob Engnath)